on the Move with JESUS

WESLEY T. RUNK

Lima, Ohio
C.S.S. Publishing Company

ON THE MOVE WITH JESUS

O87 2T

1511/ISBN 0-89536-670-3   PRINTED IN U.S.A.

TABLE OF CONTENTS

Foreword

What child doesn't love to hear a story?

These short "parables-from-life" are based on Epistle ("Second Lesson") scripture texts, and are designed to be presented by the pastor or a worship leader, either at the worship service or at Sunday church school, vacation Bible school, or children's worship time. Each makes use of some common, everyday item.

None of the messages are intended to be presented just as they are written. In fact, none of us *talk* the way we *write*. The storyteller will want to read the Scripture text and the story and (if necessary) rehearse it, until it can be presented in a natural, story-telling way.

Often tellers of children's messages forget that they are speaking, *not to the adults* who also happen to be present (even though the adults properly are "overhearing" everything). First and primarily the message is a message *to the children* who are gathered in the chancel, or wherever the story is being told. The story-teller will want to be certain that the youngest child who comes to listen can understand what is being said. If eyes and hands begin to stray, make it simpler still (and, perhaps, be prepared to depart from your "learned script" long enough to regain every youngster's attention).

All the stories in this book can be used in any Christian congregation. While some congregations do not follow a Scripture lectionary, and may choose from the contents at random, those in a liturgical pattern will find the small-type designations helpful which appear in the upper right hand corner of each title page (for congregations following the lectionary, the messages can most appropriately be used on the Sunday of the church year indicated).

Now, get ready to invite the youngsters, and to say, "Good morning, boys and girls . . ."

God Is Fair
Acts 10:34-38

Vs. 34: And Peter opened his mouth and said, "Truly I perceive that God shows no partiality."

Object: A referee's shirt and whistle.

Good morning, boys and girls. Happy New Year!! I haven't seen most of you since we started our new year. Isn't it great? We can start all over again and everything is fresh and wonderful. I hope that you have all decided to do everything right. Every night you are going to do your homework, pay attention to what your teachers tell you, come to church every Sunday, help your mom with the dishes and keep your room clean. If you do all those things you will make a lot of people happy. How many of you have decided to make other people happy? *(Let them answer.)* That's great.

All of us want to make others happy and treat everybody fair. Do you like people to treat you fair? *(Let them answer.)* What do you think it means when you say "treat people fair"? *(Let them answer.)* Most of us think that being fair means to treat everyone the same. How many of you think that God is fair? *(Let them answer.)* All of you think that God is fair.

I have a shirt and a whistle this morning that I hope you know something about. *(Show them the shirt.)* What do we call this kind of a shirt? Who wears it? *(Let them answer.)* That's right, a referee. What does a referee do? *(Let them answer.)* He makes sure that the game is played fair. Does he have a favorite team? *(Let them answer.)* Does he root for one team against another? *(Let them answer.)* No!!! He better not. If he is a good referee, he does not have a favorite team and he is fair to whoever is playing the game. The referee shows no partiality. That is a big word but an important one. Can you say it with me? Partiality.

The Bible teaches us that God shows no partiality. God is always fair. God treats you and all of your friends the same. God does not have favorites. He doesn't like you better than he likes her. God is the best referee in the whole world.

Peter found this out one day when he was thinking about God and he told everyone that he knew about it. Some people used to think that they were special to God because they lived in a certain place or had a special father and mother. Peter said no, that isn't right. God treats all people the same and loves everyone and not some people more than other people.

The next time you go to a game or watch one on TV and you see a referee with this kind of a shirt on and blowing his whistle you can think about how God is fair to all and loves everyone the same. That is something for us all to remember.

How Special You Are!
1 Corinthians 6:12-20

Vss. 19-20: Do you not know that your body is a temple of the Holy Spirit within you, which you have from God? You are not your own; you were bought with a price. So glorify God in your body.

Object: A brand new dress, suit, or some very special piece of clothing.

Good morning, boys and girls. Isn't this a wonderful Sunday morning? *(Let them answer.)* Everything seems to be just right with the world and all of you look so good. I brought along with me some very special things that I have seen in the store and I thought that you would like to look at them with me. I think that they are about the most beautiful clothes that I have ever seen. They are special because they are to be worn to some special place. Maybe they are for a party or a wedding. You can see that you would not wear this kind of a dress to clean the house or go outside and play in it. It's so bright and cheerful looking that you just know that the person who wears a dress like this is going to be beautiful in it. And how about this suit? Not everyone has a suit like this. I suppose you might wear a suit that is this special to a wedding or a very special dance. The person who wears this will also be special to look at when he has this on.

Clothes are important because they tell us something about the importance of the places that we are going to when we wear them. But the Bible tells us that there is something a lot more special than the clothes we wear. Do you know what is more important than clothes? *(Let them answer.)* All those things are important, but the Bible tells us that our own bodies are more important than any clothes. St. Paul wrote that our bodies are like temples because the Holy Spirit lives in our bodies. Did you know that God the Holy Spirit is alive within you? *(Let them answer.)* That's right, God lives in you and that makes your body a very special thing to take care of in a very special way. St. Paul calls your body a temple. Do you know what a temple is? *(Let them answer.)* A temple is like a church. It is a holy place where people believe they can talk and listen to God. Your body is a place like a temple. You speak to God and listen to God when he talks to you. That means that your body is such a special place that you should take care of it in a very special way. Don't do anything to your body that hurts it. Always do good things for your body because the Holy Spirit of God is living inside of you.

The next time you see some clothes that really seem special, and you would like to wear them to make you feel special, think about how special you already are since your body is a temple and the Holy Spirit lives in you. Amen.

Time Is Running Out
1 Corinthians 7:29-31

Vs. 29a: I mean, brethren, the appointed time has grown very short.

Object: A new bar of soap and a very used bar of soap.

Good morning, boys and girls. I brought along with me a couple of friends that most of you probably know but you don't talk to very often. How many of you have ever met Billy Big Bar and his older brother Larry Little Bar? Billy and Larry are good friends but Billy worries a lot about Larry. Every day when they wake up, Billy looks at Larry and becomes very sad. Do you know why Billy is sad about Larry? *(Let them answer.)* That's right, Larry is smaller today than he was yesterday. Do you know why? *(Let them answer.)* That's right, someone used Larry and there is less of him today than there was yesterday. One day something is going to happen that is going to make Billy very unhappy if he doesn't learn something that he doesn't know right now. Do you know what is going to happen to Larry that could make Billy sad? *(Let them answer.)* That's right, Larry is going to disappear. He is going to be gone forever. Would that make you sad if you were Larry's little brother? *(Let them answer.)*

Maybe it would, but it shouldn't. We must remember that this is the way that Larry and Billy were made, and some day the same thing is going to happen to Billy. It is a plan for soap to be used up and someday to be all gone. Billy shouldn't feel bad, but instead he should feel good for Larry because Larry is making the plan come true.

That is the same way for us. When God made the world that we live in, he knew that there was another world and that we would not stay here forever. Our world is like a piece of soap. Someday it is going to be all used up and we will disappear from this world just like Larry Little Bar is going to disappear. But it will be the way that God has planned it and therefore it will be good.

You and I are not going to live forever. Someday we will die according to the plan. Everyone else will die also. They will be used up just like us. The world that we live in will be used up and it will sort of die. But God has a bigger plan and a better plan for all of us and for all of his world. The time is always closer to the end but none of us knows when the end will come. We must trust that God will take good care of us and make us part of his new world when it is finished. Amen.

Of Backs and Cracks
1 Corinthians 8:1-13

Vs. 9: Only take care lest this liberty of yours somehow become a stumbling block to the weak.

Object: A string that could look like a crack in the sidewalk.

Good morning, boys and girls. Today I need your help. I want you to use your imagination. Do you know what I mean when I say imagination? *(Let them answer.)* That's right, I want you to pretend.

I have a string with me that I am going to lay down on the floor. We are going to pretend that the floor is a sidewalk and the string is a crack in the sidewalk. How many of you have ever seen a sidewalk cracked? *(Let them answer.)* Does the string look like a crack? *(Let them answer.)* Good, then this will help you to pretend.

There is an old saying that goes like this, "If you step on the crack, you will break your mother's back." That is an old saying and I don't believe it, do you? *(Let them answer.)* You can't break your mother's back by stepping on a crack in the sidewalk. But some people believe things like this. They think it is unlucky to step on cracks, and that if they do, something bad will happen to their mother. It won't happen, but they think it will.

You and I could step on cracks all day long and nothing would happen to anyone's mother because we stepped on the crack. But even so, it is important for us to think about. Suppose you were with a friend and he thought that stepping on that crack would hurt his mother. What would you do? *(Let them answer.)* That's right, you would try to convince him that it just couldn't happen. But he wouldn't believe you. Then, what would you do? Would you step on it a bunch of times and run home to show him that it didn't make any difference? *(Let them answer.)* I don't think so. That would just make him mad at you, and nothing good would happen. We don't want to make people mad or angry at us. That is not the way that we teach boys and girls about Jesus.

We teach about Jesus by doing good for them and not by trying to prove everything that we think is right and making them angry. St. Paul had things like this happen to him. He told all the Christians to be very concerned about people who did not know Jesus and to help them learn without making them mad.

You and I have to do the same thing. Don't try to always be right about everything when you know it makes others mad. Listen to them and try to understand them and love them a lot and they will come to know the truth by learning.

Thank you for coming this morning and thank you for letting me use your imagination. Amen.

The Man Who Brought People to Jesus
1 Corinthians 9:16-23

Vs. 22b: I have become all things to all men, that I might by all means save some.

Object: A pocket knife with many parts.

Good morning, boys and girls. How many of you have ever seen a pocket knife that looks like this? *(Hold up your special pocket knife.)* Isn't this something? Let's take a close look at it and see if you can tell me what all of the parts of this knife are used for? *(Take out each part and identify it, then put it back.)* Just imagine what you could do with a knife like this! You could cut wood, screw screws, take out corks, eat beans out of a can and I suppose help yourself with a hundred other things. This is quite a knife. It is about the best kind of knife I have ever seen. There isn't anything that you can't do with a knife like this.

St. Paul would have loved this knife. He was always trying to be to people what this knife was to other knives. Some knives can only cut, but this knife can do almost anything that you want it to do. St. Paul was that kind of a man to other men. He was a great student to other students and a hard worker to men who worked hard. He could speak many languages so that almost everyone could understand him. He knew how to live with the rich and the poor. St. Paul was quite a man and he did all the things that he did for one reason. How many of you know why St. Paul was the kind of man that he was? *(Let them answer.)* St.

Paul was this kind of a man so that he could tell everyone about Jesus and show them how Jesus helps them. He taught the rich and the poor. He taught the very smart and the very dumb about Jesus. There was not a man who was too old or a child too young that Paul did not help to learn about Jesus.

St. Paul said that he was all things to all men. He would do anything to make Jesus real to all the people in the world.

That's why I think that St. Paul is like my knife. My knife has many parts and it can do almost anything for me. I don't need another knife when I have this one. It can do anything that I ask of a knife. People didn't need another teacher when St. Paul was around. If they wanted to make a tent he would make it. If they wanted to speak Greek or Hebrew or any other language, St. Paul would speak with them. If they needed food or clothes he would get it for them. St. Paul was a great missionary for Jesus because he was all things to all people.

The next time you see a knife, maybe you will think of mine, and it will help you to remember our friend and great teacher of Jesus, St. Paul. Amen.

Exercise Your Faith in Jesus!
1 Corinthians 9:24-27

Vs. 27: But I pommel my body and subdue it, lest after preaching to others I myself should be disqualified.

Object: An exercise bicycle or some form of exercise equipment.

Good morning, boys and girls. I brought along something that many of you have seen but I wonder how many of you have used? *(Show them the exercise bicycle.)* How do you like this for a bike? *(Let them answer.)* You can't go very far on a bike like this but it is a great thing to have. How many of you know what a bike like this is good for? *(Let them answer.)* That's right, exercise. You can't ride to the grocery or down to the park on a bike like this, but if you want to have some exercise in your bedroom or family room, then this is a great thing to have. I like to use it late at night when I am watching some television or in the morning before I eat my breakfast. Do you think that this is fun? *(Let them answer.)* It is hard work. I ride that bike until I am really sweating. It makes me use all the muscles in my legs, and my heart has to beat extra fast, and when I am done riding I feel like I have been riding up hill all day long. That is quite a workout. I do it because I want to keep my body and my heart in shape. That way I will live longer and be able to enjoy life better.

St. Paul thought this was a good thing to do. St. Paul used to exercise and he knew how important it was for him to keep in shape. But he also knew that his body was not the only thing that he had to keep in shape. St. Paul was a great believer in keeping his mind in shape and practicing hard to live the kind of life that Jesus taught us to live. Paul would work hard loving those who hated him. When people tried to hurt him or say evil things about him, he would not fight back with angry words. Paul practiced what we call self control. Paul was always in charge of his body and his mind so that he would not fall into sin.

That is something that all of us can do like Paul did. We all exercise because we know that it is good for our bodies. We should also exercise our love for God so that we do not do things with our hearts, our minds or our mouths that cause us to sin. If we practice being the way Jesus taught us to be, then we wili have the strength to do the right things when we are tested.

It is easy to tell someone else how to be, but we have to be able to do it ourselves if it really counts. If I have an exercise bike and I don't use it it will not do me any good. If I tell other people how to live but I don't live that way, it will not do any good either. I must live my life the way that I practice it if I am going to help others learn to love Jesus as much as I say that I do. Amen.

2/20/00

A Guarantee From Jesus
2 Corinthians 1:18-22

Vs. 22: He has put his seal upon us and given us his Spirit in our hearts as a guarantee.

Object: A guarantee that you received with a purchase that you have recently made.

Good morning, boys and girls. How many of you have been shopping with your mom and dad when they have bought something pretty important? *(Let them answer.)* What did they buy? *(Let them answer.)* Those are important things, and I am sure that they also asked for something that I have in my hands with me right now when they made their purchase. Do you know what this is called? *(Let them answer.)* That's right, a guarantee. Do you know what a guarantee is? *(Let them answer.)* That's right, it is a piece of paper that says that the thing you bought will do what the man who sold it to you said it would do, or you get your money back. We like guarantees and they are important for us to keep when we receive them.

Jesus has made us a lot of promises. He has told us that we are his brothers and that the Father in heaven will love us like his sons. Jesus told us that there are other promises like the forgiveness of sins, and that there is a heaven where we will live with God forever. God is close to us just as Jesus promised, and we should live like it. Those are the promises that Jesus made but how do we know that they are true? That is one of the questions that St. Paul asked himself, and he got an answer. The answer is that

Jesus also gave us a guarantee. Did you hear what the guarantee is when I read the lesson this morning? *(Let them answer.)* The guarantee is the Holy Spirit that lives in our hearts. Jesus would not leave us with just a promise. He put his own spirit in our hearts so that we would know that the promise is true. A promise is something that we have to wait for to have it happen but the warm feeling that we have when we hear the name of Jesus comes from the Spirit that is in our hearts. How many of you can feel the Spirit of Jesus inside of you? *(Let them answer.)* It isn't something that you can touch but you just know that it is there. That is the guarantee. It is like having a piece of paper in your hand that tells you what you bought, promising that it will work.

Jesus tells us that we should forgive sins that people do to us and God will forgive our sins. We forgive others, but how do we know that God will forgive us? The way we know it is true is because of the way we feel inside when we tell someone that he is forgiven. And the feeling we have inside is the Spirit of Jesus telling us that everything is true and real with God.

We have our guarantee from Jesus just like this piece of paper, only the guarantee from Jesus is more important. You think about this and see if you can't feel that Spirit inside of you. Will you do that? Good. Amen.

Changing in the Spirit
2 Corinthians 3:12-4:2

Vs. 18: And we all, with unveiled face, beholding the glory of the Lord, are being changed into his likeness from one degree of glory to another; for this comes from the Lord who is the Spirit.

Object: A heating pad.

Good morning, boys and girls. How many of you have a heating pad? *(Let them answer.)* Aren't they great? I think a heating pad when you are sick is one of the best things that I know. As a matter of fact it seems to make you feel better than all of the medicine. Do you remember the last time you had a cold and you felt just terrible? Shivering one minute and so very hot the next that you knew something had to be wrong. After your mother gave you medicine she might have asked you if you would like the heating pad. The best part of the heating pad is the little switch that comes with it. Sometimes you put the pad on your cold feet and sometimes you like to lay it under you, but you always hold on to the switch. Do you remember what the switch looks like? *(Let them answer.)* That's right, it usually has colors and one of them is hotter than the rest. You can have it on warm, pretty warm or hot. You can change it by degrees. Most people start out with "hot" and then change it to pretty warm and then back to nice, plain warm. You keep changing the heat by degrees with that little switch. How many of you remember that switch? *(Let them answer.)*

Did you know that Jesus is changing you by degrees just like you change the heating pad by degrees? Did you know that his Spirit was changing you everyday so that you will be a little more like him all of the time? That's right. God is working on you through the Spirit to change you a little bit by a little bit so that you are becoming more like him every day. Isn't that great? We are changing by degrees. Do you remember the heating pad and how you would push the switch and you would never know when it got a little cooler or a little hotter but it just all of a sudden was not as hot or not as cold as it was before you moved the switch? That is the way the Spirit of God is working inside of you. Everyday that you learn and practice the things Jesus teaches you, you find that you are becoming more like Jesus. I think that is wonderful and I am sure that you think so too.

The next time you take a look at your heating pad, look at the switch and see what I mean. Turn it on to warm first, and then move it up. You will not know when it got hot, but pretty soon you will feel the difference. You have changed the heat by degrees. The Spirit of God is changing you and making you more like the Lord Jesus every day. That is one of the ways God works, and I think it is one of the best. Amen.

Throw Your Worries to the Lord
Romans 8:31-39

Vs. 35a: Who shall separate us from the love of Christ?

Object: Some business forms with carbon paper separating each sheet.

Good morning, boys and girls. It is time for us to think about some different things. Here we are in church on the first Sunday of a brand new month. Does anyone know what month this is? *(Let them answer.)* That's right, March, and what does March make you think about? *(Let them answer.)* I think about the wind and how hard it blows in the month of March. I also think about spring and how soon it will be with us. But today I am thinking about Lent. This is the first Sunday of Lent. How many of you know something about Lent? *(Let them answer.)* This is a time of year when we think about Jesus and how he suffered and died for our sins. How many of you have thought about that today? *(Let them answer.)*

We have a lot of things to think about, don't we? I think about spring and I think about my friends. I like to think about good things but sometimes I worry about being sick or having people angry with me for something. When I think about the things that cause me a lot of worry I seem to forget about Jesus. How many of you ever forget about Jesus? It seems like when we are worrying or forgetting about Jesus, we feel separated from him. Let me show you what I mean. *(Take out your carbon forms.)* Let's pretend that this first sheet of paper I have with me is Jesus, and the black piece of paper is one of my worries. Let's call this worry a friend who is mad at me. The next sheet of paper is me. *(Hold up next set of forms.)* Then I have the worry of getting real sick, and then there is me. Just think of how far I am getting away from Jesus. I am being separated from Jesus. Jesus is way up front and I am getting further and further away because of all my worries. That's bad. That's real bad. When you get that far away from Jesus you may be afraid that Jesus will forget you. But before you worry about Jesus forgetting you, let me show you something. I am going to have Jesus write you a note. Remember I told you that Jesus was the first page. Well, Jesus is writing you a note that says I love you. *(Write it out on the page.)* Now let's see if Jesus got through your worries. Here is your worry about the friend who is mad at you. We will look under that worry and see what is there. The next page is you. Look at this, the message from Jesus is written on you. Let's look at the next worry. That was our fear of getting real sick. Let's look at you under that worry. Jesus got through that worry also. His message is there. He loves you. Nothing can separate you from the love of Jesus. All your worries are not big enough to keep Jesus from you. That's something to remember. If you remember that Jesus will always be with you, you can forget about your worries because he cares for you. Will you remember? I hope so. Amen.

You're Worth a Million
Romans 5:1-11

Vs. 8: But God shows his love for us in that while we were sinners Christ died for us.

Object: A make believe check for $1,000,000.00 and an old rag.

Good morning, boys and girls. Today I am going to show you something that you won't believe, but it's true. I have a check here for $1,000,000.00 and I am going to spend it in just a few minutes. Do you know how much money $1,000,000.00 is? *(Let them answer.)* What do you think $1,000,000.00 would buy? *(Let them answer.)* A million dollars is more money than I have ever seen.

I want you to look at something else I brought with me today. Do you see this old rag I have in my hand? It isn't very pretty. I guess you wouldn't even dust your house with a rag like this, would you? *(Let them answer.)* Would anyone wear it for a shirt? *(Let them answer.)* You wouldn't wear it or use it. It is ready to be burned or thrown away in some garbage can. That means the rag is in pretty bad shape, doesn't it? *(Let them answer.)*

Guess what? I am going to spend my check for a million dollars to buy this rag. That's right, this is the reason that I brought my check for $1,000,000.00. I want to buy this rag with all the money that I have ever seen. Would you do that? *(Let them answer.)* You wouldn't do it, would you? You think I am silly, don't you? *(Let them answer.)* Well maybe I am, but I want to tell you that I am not the only one that people think is silly.

You think about spending $1,000,000.00 for a rag while I tell you something else. Did you know that God spent more than that for something that was worth about as much as my old rag? *(Let them answer.)* That's right. God gave Jesus to the world for raggedy old sinners. Would you die for a million dollars? If I put a million dollars in your bank account would you die? *(Let them answer.)* Of course you wouldn't. But God took a look at us and he saw a bunch of raggedy old people. Then he thought about how much he loved us and he decided to give the life of Jesus for all of us. He had Jesus die so that we would have all of our sins against him forgiven. Jesus paid for our sins with his life. We were filled with sin and God forgave all of us for the price of Jesus' life.

That's how much God loves us. More than a million dollars for a rag! That's nothing. Jesus gave something more than a million dollars for us. He gave us his life.

The next time you see a rag or hear about a million dollars, I want you to think about what God spent to forgive you and me for our sins. That was really spending, and it means that you are worth more than a million dollars to God. Amen. Suggestion: Be sure to void your million dollar check.

Is Jesus a Stumbling Block?
1 Corinthians 1:22-25

Vs. 23: But we preach Christ crucified, a stumbling block to Jews and folly to Gentiles.

Object: A carpenter's saw horse.

Good morning, boys and girls. I want to share a problem with you this morning. How many of you like problems? *(Let them answer.)* We all like problems we can solve, but there are not many of us who like problems that we cannot find answers to in a short period of time. I can't fix my car when it doesn't work, and I don't like that kind of a problem. I have the same kind of problem when my radio or TV is broken. I can't make them work. St. Paul had another word for problems that I like, and I want to share it with you. St. Paul called problems-without-answers stumbling blocks. I don't know what a stumbling block looked like to St. Paul, but it could have been something like this. *(Show them the carpenter's horse.)* Suppose you were walking in a dark room and you ran into this thing. What do you think would happen? *(Let them answer.)* That's right, you would probably fall over it. This horse, that's what carpenter's call it, would keep you from getting to where you are going. You would fall or trip over this stumbling block.

Paul said that Jesus being crucified was a stumbling block for many of the people he knew. People could not believe that their sins were forgiven because Jesus died on the cross. It was not logical. How could Jesus being crucified help forgive their sins? People like it when they hear that God is love and God is forgiving, but how could Jesus dying like a criminal help them be saved? That was a problem. People whom Paul knew thought that they were saved when they learned all the great teachings of Jesus and knew how to use them. That kind of learning and understanding is called wisdom. People were saved by law or wisdom. That's what they believed. The idea of Jesus being crucified and dying for their sins was impossible to them. Paul said it was a stumbling block. They tripped over the crucifixion and they never went any further.

We know differently today. It was God's plan to have Jesus die for our sins. We all break God's law and we will never know enough about anything to save ourselves. But when we trust in Christ and his dying for our sins, then we are saved to live forever with God in his world.

Believing in Jesus, and Jesus crucified, may be a stumbling block for some but not for us. We thank God for his plan to save us through Jesus. Amen.

The Powerful Gift of Faith
Ephesians 2:4-10

Vs. 8: For by grace you have been saved through faith; and this is not your own doing, it is the gift of God.

Object: A car jack.

Good morning, boys and girls. I brought with me this morning something that I call Faith. It is a nickname that I gave to something that we all have and sometimes need. Let me show you what I mean. *(Bring out the tire jack.)* How many of you know what Faith does? *(Let them answer.)* That's right, Faith is a jack. You need Faith when you have a flat tire or you need to lift your car. Have you ever tried to lift a car? *(Let them answer.)* How did you do? *(Let them answer.)* It's pretty hard to lift a car, isn't it? As a matter of fact it is impossible to hold a car up in the air while you change a tire. Just imagine that you were out on a lonely road and your car had a flat tire. You would get out of the car, look in the trunk and take out your spare tire. But you don't have a jack. There is no jack. You must lift the car to change the tire. That is impossible. You need Faith. Faith is my car jack. Faith is smaller than I. Faith doesn't weigh as much or have as much muscle, but Faith is a wonderful gift. Faith can lift my car and I can't. When Faith is lifting my car, I can change my tire and when I don't have Faith I can't.

There is another kind of Faith. Faith that is a gift from God. God gives us faith so that we can believe that God loves us and saves us. We could not believe in God if we did not have faith. Faith helps us believe that Jesus died for our sins, forgives us when we do wrong and many other things. Faith is a gift, a free gift from God and we use it everyday.

I could not lift my car without a jack. I would stand beside my car forever and it would not change. I could eat all the Wheaties, take all the vitamins I could find and I could not lift my car. It takes my car jack to lift the car. That is why I call it Faith.

You have the same gift from God. You have faith which lets you believe all that God teaches you. That is why you can believe because you have faith.

The next time you see someone lift his car to change a tire with a car jack, you can think about my jack called Faith. Then you will also remember how it takes faith to believe and how faith is a gift that comes from God. Amen.

25

Suffering . . . A Good Teacher
Hebrews 5:7-9

Vs. 8: Although he was a Son, he learned obedience through what he suffered.

Object: A policeman's ticket for speeding.

Good morning, boys and girls. Do you know what today is? *(Let them answer.)* That's right, it is Sunday, but did you all know that you have big green spots on your faces? *(Let them answer.)* Did you also know that school has been cancelled for the rest of the year and that all of you must find a job tomorrow? *(Let them answer.)* Now do you know what day it is? That's right, April Fool's Day. Did you play any tricks on your mom or dad? April Fool's Day is a lot of fun. You have to think all day long so that you will not be tricked by someone.

I have something with me this morning that is not a trick. *(Hold up the speeding ticket.)* Have you ever seen one of these? *(Let them answer.)* This is a speeding ticket. A policeman gave me one of these because he said I was driving too fast in the city. I sure didn't like the way he told me that I had to slow down while driving in the city. Of course, the thing that I didn't like the most was the idea that it is going to cost me a lot of money when I go to court. Then the judge will give me a big talk, and I will have to listen and promise him that I won't drive the way I was driving in the city. Even after the talk the judge gives me, I will still have to pay the fine. That kind of driving sure does make me suffer and suffer a lot. How do you think you would feel if you were arrested by a policeman, made to go to court, and then pay a big fine for driving a little bit too fast? Pretty bad, that's how you would feel. But you learn a lot when you suffer. I don't drive as fast in the city as I used to drive.

We all learn to obey by suffering. Sometimes our moms and dads make us suffer to teach us to obey. The policeman made me suffer and now I obey the speed laws. Suffering may hurt for a little while but if it teaches us to obey, then it is worthwhile. Maybe the next time you think you are suffering too much, you will remember how Jesus suffered for us, and then you will be thankful for his obeying the Father. Amen.

The Secret of Wally Wheelbarrow
Philippians 2:5-11

Vs. 7: But emptied himself, taking the form of a servant, being born in the likeness of men.

Object: A wheelbarrow.

Good morning, boys and girls. I brought along one of our friends today that I thought you would enjoy seeing. Do you remember Wally Wheelbarrow? *(Let them answer.)* Wally is a fine fellow. How many of you have ever worked with Wally? *(Let them answer.)* What did you do with Wally? *(Let them answer.)* You hauled dirt in Wally. Some of you picked up rocks and a few of you have even carried some wood in Wally. Wally Wheelbarrow has been a lot of places and has done a lot of things. A lot of people don't take care of Wally and they let him sit outside when it rains and he fills up with water and gets rusty. Wally doesn't like to be rusty but there isn't much he can do about it. Some other people I know let Wally sit for days with a load of dirt or rocks and they forget to empty him. That hurts Wally because Wally can't work when he is full of water, dirt or rocks. Wally has to be empty before he can be used. That's the secret with Wally. You keep emptying Wally and he will keep working for you, but if you let him stand full of something he can't do a thing.

The best part of Wally is that he likes to be used. Did you know that Wally and Jesus were a lot alike in this way? Jesus was the Son of God and because he was the Son of God he was filled with all kinds of things. Jesus knew everything there was to know.

Jesus was filled with power and there wasn't anything that he could not do. But because Jesus was coming to save us from our sins, he had to be one of us. He could not be a superman, he had to be like you and me. Jesus could not be God while he was here on earth so he emptied himself and became our servant. That's why I said that Jesus was a lot like Wally Wheelbarrow. Wally can't serve us when he is full of things and Jesus cannot be our servant when he is filled with God. Both of them have to be empty if they are to be our servants.

That is what the Bible teaches us and it is something for us to remember. We wonder why Jesus let men kill him on a cross when we know he had such great power. We wonder why he let men make him suffer when he could have stopped it in a minute. But Jesus emptied himself of all God's powers so that he could be like one of us and know what it is like to be a man or a woman, a boy or a girl. Jesus was helpless when he was empty and he was hurt because of it. But he was glad to be empty so that he could be our servant and die for our sins.

The next time you see our friend Wally I hope that he is empty and if he is, then you can think about why Jesus emptied himself so that he could be our Savior. Amen.

Lord of Light and Life
1 Corinthians 15:19-28

Vs. 21:For as by a man came death, by a man has come also the resurrection of the dead.

Object: Two buckets of water.

Good morning, boys and girls and a very happy Easter to all of you. What a day this is for all of us who believe that Jesus Christ is risen from the dead. Just think, one day Jesus was dead and lying in a grave, and the next day he was alive again, walking and talking to people he knew and loved. It is a great day and one that we never forget.

One of the things about Jesus coming back to life that is so great is that he came back to life as a man. He didn't come as a ghost or some kind of big smoke, he came back to life as a man. It was a man who committed the first sin that brought death into the world. Do you remember the story in the Bible about Adam and Eve and how they broke their promises to God? *(Let them answer.)* When they broke their promises they also brought death as a part of life. Let ɔ show you what I mean. *(Bring out the buckets filled with water.)*

I have a couple of buckets filled with water. One of these buckets I keep filled so that I can kill a fire. When I pour this bucket of water on a fire the fire dies and is gone. There is no more light or heat. The fire is cold and dead. That happened because of the bucket of water I poured on it.

Here is another bucket of water. I am going to use

this bucket of water to help grow some vegetable plants in my garden. I will water the plants very carefully so that they will grow strong in the ground. Some day I will eat the things that are grown on the plants. The water gives the plant life, and makes it strong.

The water is the same. It came from the same place, but one bucket kills and the other gives life. That is what the Bible teaches us is the difference between the man who sinned and brought death to all of us and Jesus who came and brought life to us. Easter day is the time that we celebrate the life that Jesus gave back to us after man's sin had brought us to death.

That is why we worship Jesus and show him so much love. None of us want death. All of us want life. We want more and more life and that is because God wants us to live forever. Jesus made that happen when he was resurrected and promised us that the same thing would happen to us that happened to him. We shall be like the plants in the garden that live because of the water that was shared so carefully. We shall not ever again be like the fire that was killed when the water was poured on it.

Both buckets have water. Both sin and life came from men. Only one of the men was Jesus, and he brought life to share with us forever. Amen.

31

The Family of God
1 John 5:1-6

Vs. 1: Every one who believes that Jesus is the Christ is a child of God, and everyone who loves the parent loves the child.

Object: A typewriter.

Good morning, boys and girls. I brought along my typewriter this morning so that I could share something with you that I learned while reading my Bible the other day. How many of you have ever looked closely at a typewriter? *(Let them answer.)* Did you notice all of the little keys inside? *(Let them answer.)* What is on the keys? *(Let them answer.)* That's right, there are letters on the keys. There is an a, b, c, d, e, f, g, h, i, etc. Every letter in the alphabet is on one of the keys plus some other things like numbers, periods, commas, and many other things. I like to think of those letters as though they were little people, Christian people. Each one of these people believes in God. All of the keys are like God's children. They make up a very happy family. They are like brothers and sisters to each other, but they are all different. The "e" looks different from the "y" and the "a" is different from the "m." Each letter is different, but each belongs to the alphabet family, and they are a very happy family. All of these happy letters make words and the words make sentences and the sentences make paragraphs and make the paragraphs make letters and books and sermons and many other things. My typewriter is a very happy family of letters.

God's family of Christians is also a very happy

family. It belongs together. God is like the typewriter.
People like you and me are like the letters of the
alphabet. Each one is different just like each letter is
different. Some of us are round, some of us are tall.
Some of us are black and some of us are white or
yellow or brown. But we all belong to God because we
believe that Jesus is the Christ. We are part of God's
family just like the letters are part of a letter or a book.
Now we love God a lot. He has done many wonderful
things for us. But the Bible also teaches us that if we
love God, then we must also love one another. My "y"
loves my "e" and my "l" is just wild about my "b."
Each of the letters in my typewriter love each other
because they know that they all belong to one another
and it takes all of them to make words.

You love God, and because you love God, you must
also love all the children of God who are people like
you are sitting with today, your playmates and
the people that you go to school with. When you love
God, you love all God's children who are brothers
and sisters of Jesus. Amen.

33

Let God's Light Shine
1 John 1:1-2:2

Vs. 8: If we say we have no sin, we deceive ourselves and the truth is not in us.

Object: A light bulb painted black (washable black) and a bucket of water to wash off the paint.

Good morning, boys and girls. It is getting warmer every day and soon it will be summer. How many of you remember the cold days of winter? *(Let them answer.)* It's fun to be outside without our coats and hats, isn't it? *(Let them answer.)* I love to walk in the sunshine. It seems so good. I like these days much better than the dark and cloudy ones. God must like sunshine also. The Bible speaks of God as if he were a bright light. It also talks about sin as being dark shadows.

I brought along an object today to help us understand how we can be close to God. All of us sin. Do you remember the last time that you sinned? *(Let them answer.)* When we sin it makes us dark and cloudy. We always hide our sin. We don't want other people to know that we are sinning so we try to hide it from them also. *(Take your light bulb and begin to paint it black.)* I want you to pretend that this light bulb is God and we are sinning. Do you see how we are clouding over God? The light is getting harder and harder to see. Pretty soon we will almost shut God out all together. That's the way that we feel when we sin. We are hiding from God and from his light. We don't want God to know what we are doing. We are getting

34

further and further away from him. *(Finish painting the light bulb black.)* Now that God is gone from us we feel terrible. We are in darkness. What can we do? *(Let them answer.)*

The Bible tells us that we should confess our sins. We should talk about them to God and to each other. If I have done something to you that is wrong I should tell you. I should also tell you how sorry I am. When I do this, something happens. *(Begin to wash off part of the paint.)* A little bit of light shows where we have confessed our sin. God is peeking through. There is some light coming back into our life. We feel good about this and we confess all our sins. We tell other people of the mean things that we did to them and then we confess to God about the way that we have forgotten him. Pretty soon our hearts feel different. *(Wash off all the black paint.)* The darkness of our sin is gone and the light of God is back. How much better we feel to be able to walk with God in the light.

That is what the Bible teaches us to do. We should confess our sins to God and to one another. When we do, we share our lives with him in light and we never have to live in the dark. Maybe you have something that you feel sorry about and you want to get rid of it. Tell that person you hurt and see if you don't feel the light of God all around you. I just know that you will. Amen.

Heaven Will Wait
1 John 3:1-2

Vs. 2: Beloved, we are God's children now; it does not yet appear what we shall be, but we know that when he appears we shall be like him, for we shall see him as he is.

Object: Two exact kinds of packages that do not have the picture of the product on the outside but do have some descriptive material of what is inside. Example would be some dishwashing product or some packages of nails or screws.

Good morning, boys and girls. We are going to work on a problem today. How many of you like to solve problems? *(Let them answer.)* That's good, because I like to solve problems too. It makes me feel like a good detective when I have found the answer to a big problem.

I brought along with me this morning a couple of packages. You may have seen these packages in the store, or your mom may have brought them home to use in your house. What do you notice about the packages? *(Let them answer.)* They are both packages of soap used for washing dishes. The packages are the same size and have the same name. They are both the same colors. I wonder if it says the same thing on both packages. Let's read what it says. *(Begin to read from one package then read the same sentence from the other box.)* It sounds the same on both. *(Read on from the one package and then do the same with the other package.)* Both packages seem to be the same thing. If you went into the store and bought two packages that looked exactly alike would you expect them to have

the same thing on the inside? *(Let them answer.)* You
think that they would be exactly alike. I would too. Do
you know what the things on the inside look like? *(Let
them answer.)* I don't know because I have never seen
them. But if I opened one box I could be very sure that
the same thing was in the other box and they would
look the same, right? *(Let them answer.)* You are very
good detectives. Now here is another problem. See if
you can give me the answer. What will we be like in
heaven? How will we look? What will we wear? How
old will we be? Will we live together? These questions
and a lot of other questions are the ones that we have
about heaven. We don't know the answers. But the
Bible tells us something that we can be sure about.
God made us a promise that we will be like Jesus when
he comes back. We will look like him, talk like him, act
like him, be like him. We know some things about
heaven, but we do not know much about how we will
be except that we will be like God's Son when he
comes back.

We are not ready for heaven yet. When it is time for
us to live with God, then Jesus will come, and when he
comes, we will know what he is like and then we will be
very sure of what we will be like. That's the way God
planned it and that's the way it will be. Amen.

How Do I Love You?
1 John 3:18-24

Vs. 18: Little children, let us not love in word or speech but in deed and in truth.

Object: A great big book and some special shoes.

Good morning, boys and girls. Today you are going to learn something about love. How many of you know a lot about love? *(Let them answer.)* What do you think love is all about? *(Let them answer.)* Love is pretty important, isn't it? The people whom you love are important to you and you must also be important to them. How you know that some people love you or how they know that you love them is what we are going to find out this morning.

Before we answer all of the questions about love I wanted to tell you something about me. I can do a lot of great things that you don't know about. For instance, did you know that I can read this book in 30 seconds? *(Let them answer.)* Let me show you. *(Take the book and turn the pages very fast for about 30 seconds.)* My that was a good book. I am certainly glad that I read it. Do you think that you could read a book that big so fast? *(Let them answer.)*

That is not all I can do that is very special. I have some other things that are really different. I have some special shoes, and when I put these shoes on I can walk up a wall. That wall over there would be easy if I put on my special shoes. Would you like to take a look at my special wall-walking shoes? *(Let them answer.)* So you can see that I am a very special person. I can read very fast, almost faster than anyone in the world and I can walk on walls. What do you think of me now? *(Let them answer.)* You want to see me walk up a wall? *(Make some excuses as to why you can't do that now.)*

Why can't I just tell you that I can read that fast or walk up walls? That is what we do with love. We just tell people that we love them a lot of times. We don't have to prove it. We just say, "I love you." Isn't telling people that you love them good enough? *(Let them answer.)* How could I show someone that I love him? *(Let them answer.)* In other words you have to prove to people that you love them. You do things for them, help them, forgive them, work for them and share your life with them. Love isn't just kissing and hugging, is it? Love is doing a lot of things and if you don't do them then no one is sure of your love. You are never going to believe that I can read a book that fast or walk up a wall until you see me do it, are you? *(Let them answer.)* You won't believe that I love you until I share my life with you either. The same thing is true for you. Love is not easy and it is something that we must prove to everyone. Amen.

God is Love
1 John 4:1-11

Vs. 8: He who does not love does not know God; for God is love.

Object: Some ice and some rubber balls.

Good morning, boys and girls. How many of you remember my telling you that love is doing things for one another? *(Let them answer.)* You can't just tell people that you love them, you must show them that you love them. Love is shared. When you have something that is good, you want to share it with others. Love is good, so it should be shared.

Today we are going to find out where love comes from. BUT BEFORE WE DO THAT I must show you some things that will help me show you where love comes from. First, I have something that you might use every day. You put it in a glass with water or with coke or tea. Take a very good look at what I am talking about and tell me what it is. *(Let them look at some ice cubes.)* What do we call these things? *(Let them answer.)* That's right, ice. What do we know about ice? *(Let them answer.)* That's right, it is cold. All ice is cold. The one thing that we know about ice is that it is cold. We even call other things that are very cold, "ice" cold.

The next thing that I brought with me bounces; it is played with in games where you use a bat and glove or a basket. What do we call these things? *(Let them answer.)* Yes, we call them balls. What do we know about balls that bounce? *(Let them answer.)* Very good, they are round. Ice is cold and balls are round. Ice is not warm and balls are not square. Now where does love come from? That was our question. I know that I can always find love if I look to God. God is love just like balls are round and ice is cold. The words go together. Love comes from God just like roundness comes from balls and cold comes from ice.

The Bible tells us that God is love. The Bible teaches us that God is love in the same way that a science book might tell you that ice is cold and a game book would tell you that balls are round.

God is love. The big secret that I want to share with you today is that your love comes from God. God is love and when he shares himself with you then you are filled with love. When you share your love with a friend, then you are sharing God. If I give you some ice I am giving you something cold. If you take the ice and give it to someone else then you are sharing your cold. God is love. That is where love comes from and if you want a lot of love you must receive it from God. Amen.

Practice Makes Perfect
1 John 4:13-21

Vs. 18a: There is no fear in love, but perfect love casts out fear.

Object: A balance beam (borrowed from YMCA, school, or simply a 12 foot 4 x 4 board borrowed from a lumber yard) and some bricks.

Good morning, boys and girls. Today we are going to have a special event. How many of you like to do gymnastics? *(Let them answer.)* Do you know what I mean when I talk about gymnastics? *(Let them answer.)* I watch them on TV and I love to watch all the things that the boys and girls do with their bodies. One of the favorite events in gymnastics is walking and doing things on the balance beam. *(Bring out the beam.)* This is a long piece of wood that people balance themselves on, walk, turn somersaults and do handstands. The girls who do these things are very good and they show us good balance. Have you ever walked on a balance beam? *(Let them answer.)* Would you like to try? *(Let them answer.)*

(Place the beam on the floor and let them all try to walk across it without falling.) That is very good. Now I am going to put a brick under each end and see if you can walk across without falling. *(Raise the beam with each brick, stressing the danger of going higher and higher and falling.)*

It can get pretty scary if you don't know what you are doing. That is why the people who do it on TV are always practicing. They practice hours every day on the balance beam so that they will not be afraid. The same thing is true, according to Jesus, about love.

Love improves with practice. The more that you love, the less there is to be afraid about. Love always takes you to new places. In the beginning you can only love yourself and maybe your mother and father. You are afraid to love anyone else. But every day you practice loving and want to love someone new. It is like going up higher and higher on the beam. Now you want to love your friend next door. Loving means caring about them and sharing your life with them. That is kind of dangerous if you don't know how they feel about you. You are taking a chance. But if you practice sharing and caring, then you get better at it, and you are less afraid. Pretty soon you can love the people at school like your teachers and your classmates. Someday you are going to love one person who will be your husband or wife. That is kind of scary now but if you practice your sharing and caring it will work.

Going up higher and higher on the beam may seem scary if you don't practice, just like loving your friends. But if you do practice loving every day it can be the most wonderful feeling in the whole world. Will you all practice? I hope so. Amen.

Happy Birthday, Church!
Acts 2:1-2

Vs. 2: And suddenly a sound came from heaven like the rush of a mighty wind, and it filled all the house where they were sitting.

Object: A big electric fan. Increase the sound by use of a microphone. If a fan is not available, then let the children make the noise themselves.

Good morning, boys and girls. Today is Pentecost. This is the birthday of the Church. The Christian Church was born on Pentecost Day. How many of you know when you were born? *(Let them answer.)* Everyone knows his or her birthday and today is the birthday of the Church. Let's say "Happy Birthday" to the Church. *(Lead them in saying Happy Birthday.)*

Pentecost is a great church holiday. On Pentecost we remember the very first day that the Church had life. It was a day like this. Everything was kind of quiet. The disciples of Jesus were together in an upstairs room when all of a sudden they heard a sound, a loud sound. *(Turn on the fan.)* It sounded like something they had heard before only louder than anything that they had experienced. What does that noise sound like to you? *(Let them answer.)* It sounds like a wind, a big wind, bigger than any wind they had ever heard before. Whenever something like that happens to people, people like you and me, it scares them. The disciples were afraid and they ran out of the house. There in the street the wind seemed to stop, but people were coming from everywhere.

At that time of the year there were a lot of people

come from other countries in Jerusalem. You can tell when people come from other countries because they may dress a little differently and speak differently. Have you ever heard someone speak another language? *(Let them answer.)* You can't understand them, can you? *(Let them answer.)* Usually you can't. But on this day everyone was speaking his own language and God worked a wonderful miracle. As Peter preached his special sermon, everyone understood him. Peter told everyone about Jesus and the wonderful things that he had done. He told people about how Jesus taught us of God's love, died for our sins, and rose from the grave. The people were just wild about the things that Peter said that day. Thousands of them decided to follow Jesus. They were baptized that day and made members of Christ's Church. That is why we call this the birthday of the Church. All of God's promises came true that day because the Spirit of God came to live with us. Pentecost is a day that all of us remember and the Church celebrates it today. Let's all say this together. "God bless the Father." *(Have them repeat it.)* "God bless the Son." *(Have them repeat it.)* "God bless the Holy Spirit." *(Have them repeat it.)* "And God bless the Church." *(Repeat it.)* Happy Birthday, Church. Amen.

Follow the Spirit
Romans 8:14-17

Vs. 14 For all who are led by the Spirit of God are sons of God.

Object: A needle and some thread.

Good morning, boys and girls. How many of you sew? *(Let them answer.)* It isn't easy to sew well, is it? *(Let them answer.)* What did you ever sew? *(Let them answer.)* What do you need in order to sew? *(Let them answer.)* That's right, you need a needle and some thread. Can you tell me what the needle does? *(Let them answer.)* It makes a hole in whatever you are sewing and pulls the thread through the hole.

Would you pretend with me for a minute and call our needle a leader? *(Let them answer.)* Let's watch the needle when it sews. It always goes first and the thread follows it wherever it goes. If I make a hole here the thread follows the needle. *(Make a few stitches.)* If I make another hole over here the thread follows in the same direction. The needle is the leader. We could call the Holy Spirit a needle. The Holy Spirit of God leads people to worship and to learn about God. Wherever the Spirit goes, Christians follow him. The Bible teaches us that we are doing right when we follow the Spirit.

The Spirit leads us to worship God. The Spirit brings us together like we are here this morning. We sing songs about God and listen to the words of Jesus from the Bible. It is the Spirit who brings us here. The Spirit leads us to help other people and to share the things we have with others who are less fortunate.

Sometimes the Spirit of God will lead us into a quiet room where we can pray. Other times the Spirit will lead us into the noisiest crowds where we can tell others of the great love of Jesus. But the thing that we are learning today is that the Spirit of God is the Leader. We follow him.

We are like the thread. We are important to God. We keep lots of things together. But we must always follow the needle and go where the needle takes us. The Pastor of the Church, someone like me, has to listen very carefully and prayerfully to the Spirit so that he can help you to know where you and I are going. God's Spirit is a leader.

The next time you see someone sewing and you see the needle going through the cloth I want you to think about how the needle is like the Holy Spirit of God and how we are his followers. The followers of the Holy Spirit are called the sons and daughters of God. Amen.

The Treasure Inside
2 Corinthians 4:5-12

Vs. 7: But we have this treasure in earthen vessels, to show that the transcendent power belongs to God and not to us.

Object: A cigar box with jewelry and money.

Good morning, boys and girls. Today we want to talk a little bit about the way God shares all his wonderful blessings with us. I have always thought that it was pretty nice of God to share his world with me. He could have chosen the animals or the plants to share his story with but he chose people. The Bible talks about it in another way. Let me show you what I mean.

Let's suppose that you and I are really cigar boxes. Has anyone ever called you a cigar box? *(Let them answer.)* I didn't think so. But I want you to pretend that you are an old cigar box. Do you have any old cigar boxes at home? *(Let them answer.)* What do you use them for? *(Let them answer.)* For junk, right! I keep old screws and nails in one cigar box. In another one there are string, washers, old paint brushes and a lot of rust and dirt. There is nothing very valuable in a cigar box. Just suppose that you are one of God's cigar boxes and he has chosen you to carry something around for him. What do you think God would put in you if you were one of his old cigar boxes? *(Let them answer.)*

Well, the truth of the matter is that God thinks you are a pretty neat cigar box. If we open the cigar box that I have brought and pretend that this is really you, we find that he has put all his jewels inside of you.

48

(Show them the cigar box with all the beautiful jewelry that you can find and some big money.) Wow, what a cigar box. Have you ever seen one like this around your house? Look at the jewels and the money. If you are God's old cigar box you are really something according to God. He has trusted you with the best that he has. Of course God doesn't put jewels and money inside of us, but he does trust us with the best that he has.

Just think, he gave you the story of all of his heroes to remember. He shared with us his law like the Ten Commandments. He gave us the life of Jesus to keep for ourselves and also to share with others. He taught us how to pray and to forgive. He gave us a place in which to live, all his sunshine, food, and everything else that is really important. All these things he put into people like you and me. We may look like old cigar boxes, but we are really something to God.

The next time that you see an old cigar box I hope it reminds you of this one that I have with me today. When you see it you will say, "I am one of God's cigar boxes and that makes me someone really special. I have all God's favorite things inside of me and I can share what he has given with all my friends." Will you do that too? Wonderful! Amen.

A Great Big Bunch of Love
2 Corinthians 4:13-18

Vs. 18: Because we look not to the things that are seen but to the things that are unseen; for the things that are seen are transient, but the things that are unseen are eternal.

Object: An invisible "armful" of love.

Good morning, boys and girls. How are you on this special day? *(Let them respond.)* Do you know what day this is? *(Let them tell you.)* Right. This is Father's Day. Today we are especially nice to our fathers because today we want to thank them for all of the wonderful things they do. I have a great gift with me today, boys and girls, which you could give to your dads. Would you like to see it? *(Let them respond.)* Well, here it is. How do you like it? *(Hold your arms out, as if holding a huge package. Let the children respond.)* Can't you see this gift? *(Let them respond.)* Why, this is the best gift of all. Let me tell you about it, then maybe you will be able to see what it is. This gift could make all of the troubles in the world go away! Wouldn't that be wonderful, boys and girls? You see, this gift is sort of catching. You know how you can catch a cold or the measles from someone else? Well, when you give this gift away, it spreads, and other people catch it, too. Can you guess how big this gift is? *(Let them guess.)* Well, this gift can be as big as you want it to be. It will be at least as big as your heart. Another wonderful thing about this gift is that it will last forever if you want it to. How long do your toys usually last after Christmas Day? *(Let them respond.)* Sometimes your Christmas presents don't even make it to the next Christmas. Some of them get broken or lost. Some of them get too small for you. Gifts don't last a very long time, do they boys and girls? Well, this gift — if you treat it right — will last forever! You will never outgrow it. Another strange thing about this gift is that even though you give it away, you still have it! Did you ever give someone a present that you really wanted yourself? *(Let them answer.)* It is really hard to give away something that you like very much. Well, with this gift, even though you give it away, you still have it! Can anyone see what this gift is? *(Let them guess.)* This wonderful gift is **love**. Even though you can't touch it or weigh it or put it in a box, it is very real, isn't it, boys and girls? *(Let them respond.)* Your parents give you lots of love each day. Because love is catching, you have lots of it now that you can give to other people. Who are some of the people that would like a little bit of your love? *(Let them answer.)* Those are good people to share your love with, boys and girls. Most of all, on this Father's Day, let's all give a great big bunch of love to our dads so that they will know how much we care about them. Will you do that, boys and girls? Good. So will I. God bless you. Amen.

God's Guarantee
2 Corinthians 5:1-10

Vs. 5: He who has prepared us for this very thing is God, who has given us the Spirit as a guarantee.

Object: A Good Housekeeping seal, a guarantee.

Good morning, boys and girls. Isn't this a wonderful day, the first day of July? How many of you know what holiday we will celebrate this week? *(Let them answer.)* That is right. The Fourth of July. What do you like most about the Fourth of July? *(Let them answer.)* Firecrackers, picnics, and maybe even swimming at the beach all sound like a lot of fun to me. It sounds to me like everyone is guaranteed a good time. How many of you know what the word "guarantee" means? *(Let them answer.)* The word "guarantee" sounds like a big word but it means that someone is promising someone else that whatever they say is really going to happen. Let me show you what I mean. There is a magazine called the *Good Housekeeping Magazine* and in it there are advertisements. Sometimes the *Good Housekeeping* places a special seal with these advertisements. This is their guarantee that whatever is in the advertisement will do exactly as it says. The *Good Housekeeping Magazine* promises you that this thing will work or they will give you your money back. God makes guarantees also. Instead of a Good Housekeeping seal, God sends us the Holy Spirit as his guarantee. God promises you and me that whatever he says to us or whatever he does for us will never fail and his spirit teaches us that truth.

God is preparing you and me for a time when we will live with him. We can't do that now. It isn't time for us to live with God in his world so he shows us how good it will be by sharing his Holy Spirit with us in our world today. When God's spirit is with us in this world it is very much like the way God will make it in the new world. The Holy Spirit makes our lives wonderful, and when you and I share our lives with him, we know that God's promise is true.

When you see the Good Housekeeping seal, you know that the magazine promises you that their advertisements are true and they work. When God's spirit teaches us a truth in the Bible, it is God's guarantee to us that whatever he says is absolutely true. Remember this: The Holy Spirit is God's guarantee and you can believe that promise as long as you live. In Christ's name. Amen.

Extra Special People
2 Corinthians 5:14-21

Vs. 16: From now on, therefore, we regard no one from a human point of view; even though we once regarded Christ from a human point of view, we regard him thus no longer.

Object: A telescope.

Good morning, boys and girls. How many of you like to look up in the sky at night and watch the stars? *(Let them answer.)* Aren't they beautiful? They form all kinds of designs in the sky. Has anyone seen the Big Dipper? *(Let them answer.)* Could you find the Little Dipper? *(Let them answer.)* Stars are really a wonderful part of God's creation. When you see a star, what does it look like to you? *(Let them answer.)* I wish you could see a star in another way. How many of you have ever seen a star through a telescope? *(Let them answer.)* It looks a lot different. It doesn't twinkle so much and sometimes it is many different colors. Some stars look more like our moon or our sun, when we see them through a telescope. The stars that we see in the sky are much bigger than the earth we live on, and many of them are hotter than fire. A star in the telescope looks a lot different than when we just look at the stars with our own eyes. The Bible teaches us that when we become Christians, we think of people much differently than we did before we were Christians. People are very precious and they are children of God. Every person is someone special to God. Some people think that Jesus was just another man who liked to teach and who liked to talk to others about God.

Christians believe that Jesus is someone extra, extra, extra special. Christians also believe that people who love God and who share with one another are also extra special because they are brothers and sisters of Jesus. When you are a Christian and you think about people, it is like looking at a star through a telescope. They look different; they are bigger and better and more wonderful. When Chrisians think of Jesus, it is also like looking at a star through a telescope. He is so special to all of us.

The next time you are outside at night and you look up into the sky and see stars, think about what we have learned this morning. Almost all the stars look alike from here, just like people whom we don't know all look alike. But remember that when you look through a telescope, the star is brighter, bigger, and perhaps has many colors, and it seems very special. When you are a Christian and you look at people, you will think that they are special also. I hope you will pretend all the time that you are looking at people through a telescope and then you will know how special they are to you, just as they are to God. Amen.

Share What You Have
2 Corinthians 8:1-9, 13-14

Vs. 14: But that as a matter of equality your abundance at the present time should supply your want, that there may be equality.

Object: Ice cube tray and a pitcher of water.

Good morning, boys and girls. We live in a wonderful land, don't we? *(Let them answer.)* We have so many things that sometimes it is hard for us to appreciate all that we have. We have food, clothes, good houses, yards to play in, parks, cars, and all sorts of other wonderful things. We have so much that we sometimes do not know what to do with it all. The Bible says we have an abundance. Abundance means more than what we need, and that's good. It is better to have more, than to have less, but not everyone has more. Some people do not have any of the things that you or I have. They are hungry, they wear rags, they don't have any yards or parks to play in. They have much less. It has almost always been like this. Even in the times of Jesus there were people with abundance, and people who had almost nothing. What should we think about a problem where some people have more than they can use and other people don't have any at all? Let me show you what I think is the answer.

(Take out the ice cube tray and the pitcher of water.) I am going to pour some water into this end of the tray and I am not going to pour any water into the other end of the tray. We will say the end of the tray with the water has an abundance. The other end has nothing. Let us see what happens. *(Pour the water into*

*the tray and let the children see how each cubicle fills
up to the same place.)* What do you think of this, boys
and girls? What has happened? *(Let them answer.)* All
of the parts now have the same amount of water. The
end with the abundance has shared with the end that
has nothing. St. Paul taught us that Christians should
learn to share their abundance with others who have
nothing. Some day the people who now have nothing
will have an abundance and they will want to share
what they have with those who may have nothing. It's a
good plan and it helps people to know each other and
love one another. The next time you see an ice cube
tray, maybe you can remember the story of how
Christians learn to share their abundance with others.
In Christ's name. Amen.

Look to the Lord
2 Corinthians 12:7-10

Vs. 9a: But he said to me, "My grace is sufficient for you, for my power is made perfect in weakness."

Object: Two different kinds of medicine and a heavy pan.

Good morning, boys and girls. How are you feeling today? *(Let them respond.)* That's good, because if you weren't, you could probably take some of this medicine here! *(Hold up the medicine.)* Did you ever see that commercial on television about the woman who has a very sore arm? In that commercial, she tells us that she has arthritis and it is very hard for her to pick up something like this pan. *(Show them the pan.)* Would one of you like to lift this pan? *(Let several children try to lift it.)* It is pretty heavy but it isn't too heavy for you, is it? Well, in the commercial, the lady with the sore arm just can't lift it. Her arms hurt too much. So guess what she is told to do? Does anyone know? *(Let them guess.)* A man with several bottles of medicine tells her to try this one special kind. So she tries it. What happens to her after she takes the medicine? *(Let them tell you.)* Right! She can lift the pan without any trouble at all! It is almost like magic, isn't it, boys and girls? The woman's pain goes away after she takes this particular pill. That must be a pretty wonderful pill, don't you agree? *(Let them respond.)* Then there is another commercial about a person who has a terrible cold. She is sitting in bed, coughing and sneezing and blowing her nose. She looks and sounds just terrible! Did you ever have a coughing-sneezing-dripping kind of cold, boys and girls? *(Let them respond.)* Well, then you know just how this lady looked and sounded. However, she sent her husband to the drug store for something very special. She knew that there was a kind of medicine which would stop her sneezing, take away her sore throat, clear up her head so she could breathe, stop her coughing, and help her to sleep. Did you ever hear of a medicine like that? *(Let them respond.)* Well, I guess this medicine really worked — at least on television, because after she took it, the lady was able to sleep. You know, sometimes we read some of St. Paul's letters during our worship service. St. Paul must have had a special problem — either a bad pain or some other kind of thing that was hard for him to live with. St. Paul doesn't tell us what it is — but apparently there weren't any special medicines for it like the ones we have today. St. Paul even talked to the Lord about it, but the Lord said not to worry. His grace would help him to stand it. Sometimes all the medicines in the world won't help us feel better, will they, boys and girls? Then we have to remember St. Paul; he just put his trust in the Lord and let the Lord take care of him. That isn't always easy for us to do, is it, boys and girls? But that's what trust and faith are all about — putting our hand in the Lord's and letting him take care of us. The next time we see one of these commercials about pills and other wonderful medicines, let's remember that sometimes we have to just look to the Lord — especially when everything else fails. God bless you, boys and girls. Amen.

Safe With the Spirit
Ephesians 1:3-14

Vs. 13: In him you also, who have heard the word of truth, the gospel of your salvation, and have believed in him, were sealed with the promised Holy Spirit.

Object: A large manila envelope.

Good morning, boys and girls. How many of you have ever used an envelope? *(Let them answer. Show them a big manila envelope.)* Have you ever written a letter or sent something to a friend through the mail and you needed an envelope? It's fun to write letters and even more fun to get them, isn't it? You can't just send the letter without an envelope. The envelope is important because whatever you put inside is kept together. If I just sent the letter without an envelope, there would be no address, the pages would come apart, or the stamp would cover part of what was said. I couldn't send a check or money without putting it in an envelope because no one would know who it was for and it would simply be lost or taken. An envelope is really a very important part of any letter that you send. The Holy Spirit is like an envelope. A Christian has many parts and all of the parts are important. A Christian learns from other Christians and from the Bible. A Christian believes many things about God and the way God loves him. A Christian shares many of the things that he has, such as money, food, clothes, and all kinds of things. But the Holy Spirit brings all of those things together and keeps them together so that none of them are lost. That's why we say the Holy Spirit is like an envelope. The Holy Spirit n   only keeps them together for you but also keeps you ,or God. The Holy Spirit promises God the Father that what you learn and what you believe and what you share will be kept forever, and the Holy Spirit doesn't do that just for you but for everyone who believes in, learns about, and shares God.

If you have ever seen a post office or if you have looked into a postman's mailbag, you will see all kinds of envelopes. The Holy Spirit shares himself with everyone. There are many hundreds, thousands, and millions of people who have learned and shared and believed in God. The Holy Spirit keeps every one of them safely for God the Father. That's his promise and he keeps it. In Christ's name, Amen.

Getting It Together
Ephesians 2:13-22

Vs. 16: And might reconcile us both to God in one body through the cross, thereby bringing the hostility to an end.

Object: A knot.

Good morning, boys and girls. How many of you would like to be a Boy Scout or a Girl Scout? Boy Scouts and Girl Scouts learn many things and have lots of exciting adventures. But one of the things they learn that I like best is how to tie knots. How many of you know how to tie a knot? *(Let them answer.)* There are all kinds of knots. There are special knots for sailors, mountain climbers, and then there are just regular knots for people like you and me. Tell me one kind of knot that you can tie. How many of you know how to tie your shoes? That takes a special kind of knot. Knots are really fun but they also tell us a very special story about the way God helps people like you and me. I brought with me today two pieces of rope. When you see what happens with these pieces of rope, you will understand something new about Jesus. This piece of rope, the big piece, is God and this piece of rope, the little piece, is you or I. The two pieces of rope can be as far apart or as close together as you want them to be. God and people are like that also. You can be as close to God as you want to be or you can live like you never heard of God. But no matter how far or how close you are to God, you are not together. You are still two pieces of rope. God had a plan, a very special plan, and he called that plan Jesus. God, the big piece of rope took ahold of a little piece of rope and made a knot with the little piece of rope. The knot is called Jesus. Jesus brings together God and people like you and me. The Bible has a special word for this knot and it is called reconciling. It means bringing two persons or things together. God brought you and me together with him in the knot called Jesus. That's a pretty wonderful plan and it makes a lot of sense. It is something that none of us could do ourselves, but only God can do.

The next time you tie a knot or you see someone else tie a knot, I hope it reminds you of this story and how Jesus is the knot that brings God and us together. In Jesus' name, Amen.

Growing In Love
Ephesians 4:1-7, 11-16

Vs. 15: Rather, speaking the truth in love, we are to grow up in every way into him who is the head, into Christ.

Object: A measuring tape.

Good morning, boys and girls. How tall are you? I mean, how tall is each one of you? Do you know how tall you are? *(Speak to one child at a time.)* How tall are you? Sometimes we know how tall we are and sometimes we just guess. But I brought with me this morning a measuring tape so I can tell you just how tall you are. Let me measure a couple of you now and after the service is over, if you would like for me to, I will measure every one of you. *(Proceed to measure several of the children and tell each one how tall he/she is.)* Have you always been that tall? Were you this big when you were born? How did you get to be as tall as you are? *(Let them answer.)* You grew. How much have you grown in the last year, would you say? *(Let them answer.)* Growing up is fun. It really is fun. Someday you are going to be as tall or taller than your mom and dad. You may weigh as much or even more. You will be big enough to drive a car, wear a suit as big as your father's suit or your mother's dress. You may even be tall enough to dunk a basketball in a 10-foot basket. That's what happens when our bodies grow and we get big. But there are other ways to grow besides just getting big in our bodies. When we learn in school, our minds grow. We can spell bigger words and do harder math problems. Our voices grow also.

They get bigger, deeper, or higher, and they will become more beautiful if we practice with them. There is still another way to grow and that is to grow in love so that our love is more like Jesus' love. Jesus was filled with God's love. He loved everyone, even those who hated him. Jesus had a love so big that he could forgive even the people that crucified him. Growing in love will let you share the things you like the most with other people. You can share your time in love. You can share your money in love. You can share your games and your friends in love. You can even share your mother and dad with other people when you are growing in love. That is a real grown-up kind of love when you can share it with others. Growing up is so much fun when it is filled with love. It allows you to be free and do what God wants you to do. A measuring tape is one way to find out how big we are getting. Three feet tall, four feet tall, five feet tall, or more means that we are eating the right kind of food and taking good care of our bodies. But growing up in love cannot always be seen so easily, but it is a much more important kind of growing than just getting tall. One of the first things that Jesus taught all of his disciples was to grow in love. And one of the things that you and I must find out who want to be followers of Jesus is to grow in love. The next time we see someone trying to find out how tall they are or to measure someone else, see if you can think about how you could measure someone growing in love. If you can see someone else grow in love, that means that you are growing in love as well. Try it, you'll like it. In Jesus' name, Amen.

A New Look
Ephesians 4:17-24

Vs. 24: And put on the new nature, created after the likeness of God in true righteousness and holiness.

Object: Pictures of before and after a house is remodeled or sided.

Good morning, boys and girls. Today we are going to talk about making old things new. We like things to look almost brand new. Look at this picture of the seen an old house made to look like a new house? *(Let them answer.)* I brought along some pictures of a house that used to look like this. *(Show them the pictures.)* It's not very pretty, is it? It looks like it needs to be painted, the windows fixed, the yard cleaned up, and a lot of different things done to it before you or I would want to live in it. I feel sorry for houses like this, don't you? It's not the way that we would like to be treated if we were a house, would we? I always think about how the house looked when it was first painted. It had people living in it who were proud to be there. You can imagine what the house looks like inside if it is this bad on the outside. But houses that look like this don't have to stay this way. They can be made to look almost brand new. Look at this picture of the same house after someone has really worked on it hard. *(Show them the picture of the remodeled house.)* Isn't it beautiful? This is the same house after men and women worked on it by painting and fixing up all of the bad places. A house is something special and is really important to a lot of people.

The Bible teaches us that people are even more

important than houses. Sometimes a person can look like an old, run-down house. Sometimes those people feel on the inside just like they look on the outside. They are run down and have no hope. But St. Paul taught us that we can be brand new when we believe in Jesus' love for us, and live the way he teaches us to live. When people like you and me love Jesus and love each other, we are more wonderful inside than we even look on the outside. Having Jesus be a part of our lives is like a fresh coat of paint, new boards, shiny windows, and all sorts of good things like that. St. Paul calls this "putting on the new nature" because he says that people who take Jesus into their lives begin to act and feel like God. The next time you are walking by an old house and you see people working on it to make it look like brand new, maybe you can think about how some people that you know could also change if you shared with them your love and the love which Jesus has given you. Putting on a new nature is even more important than having a new house. That's what the Bible says and I believe it. I hope you do too. Amen.

9/3/00

Be Imitators of the Best
Ephesians 4:30-5:2

Vs. 1: Therefore be imitators of God, as beloved children.

Object: Different brands of colas — Coke, Pepsi, Royal Crown, etc.

Good morning, boys and girls. Today I brought with me something that all of you probably like a lot. I brought different kinds of cola. I have Coca Cola, Pepsi Cola, Royal Crown Cola, and they are all favorites of mine. One of them was made first. I think it was Coca Cola and people liked it so much that soon someone made another kind and called it Pepsi Cola and pretty soon there was another and then another and then another. We will call the first one an original and all of the rest are imitators. That's not bad because people like the imitators very much. As a matter of fact, the reason that I brought all of them is that I want you to learn something about yourself and God by knowing these different kinds of colas. Let's pretend that the Coca Cola is God. God is first and God is good and because God is so good and because he loves so much, he wants us to be like him. We can't be God, but St. Paul teaches us that we can imitate him. We can try to be the way that God is. Of course, we will never be the same as God but neither is Pepsi Cola or Royal Crown Cola like Coca Cola. Being an imitator of God means that we are always ready to forgive someone who has hurt us. Being an imitator of God is like sharing what we have with everyone. Being an imitator of God means helping people to learn or helping them when they are sick or visiting them when

68

they are lonely. All of those things are the way in which we imitate God because that is the way God is. We will never have as much love or as much forgiveness or be able to heal as perfectly or take care of the lonely as well as God does, but we can try and the better we are as imitators of God the better we will be. People like you and me like not only Coca Cola, but we also like the imitators of Pepsi and Royal Crown, and we think they taste delicious. As a matter of fact, we are awfully glad that someone tried to imitate the original. The next time you see a bottle of Coke or Pepsi or Royal Crown or any other kind of cola, think about how you and I are imitators of God and how glad we are that we have God to follow to make our lives better. In Jesus' name, Amen.

Sing a Song to Each Other
Ephesians 5:15-20

Vs. 19: Addressing one another in psalms and hymns and spiritual songs, singing and making melody to the Lord with all your heart.

Object: Write out some sentences in which you greet the children of your congregation by reading to them a melody which you simply make up as you go along.

(The following is a sample of what you might use after the children are seated, and before you address them in song.) "Good morning children of St. Mark Church, and may God bless you on such a beautiful day. I thank the Lord for your joy and love which he gave you to share with your mothers and fathers and all of your friends. I praise God for our beautiful place to worship and for all of his gifts of food and energy and sunlight and rain. I pray to Jesus that we will have a wonderful time together this morning, and that the Spirit of God will go with you all this day so that your happiness will be a blessing to all that meet you wherever you walk and wherever you play."

I like to do that, and I wish I would do it more often. How do you like being greeted with a song? *(Let them answer.)* It seems a little strange, doesn't it? *(Let them answer.)* St. Paul suggested to the people in the church at Ephesus that they should always say hello to one another in this way. I don't know if they did it all the time, but it is sure a beautiful way to start the day, isn't it? When you sing songs, your heart is happy and light, and when you are happy and light, it makes the people you meet happy and light. Of course, the main reason that Paul told the people to greet each other this way was so that they could praise God and thank God for his love and the wonderful friendships that God made for people in the Church. Some of the best friends you will have will be people that you meet in church. By thanking God and saying hello to one another at the same time, we are reminded of how important God is to us and to our friendship. Of course, we don't have to make every greeting quite so long as I did this morning. You could just say, "Good morning Mark, God bless you." *(Sing to one of your children or several in this way.)* I think it is kind of fun, and it certainly does what St. Paul wanted it to, doesn't it? It makes us think of God, and it is a wonderful way to say hello to a friend.

The next time you come to Sunday School, or maybe when you see a friend today, you can try it and see how good it makes both of you feel. *(Close by singing.)* "Now thank you for coming and sharing this part of worship with me. May God bless you today in whatever you do. Amen."

9/17/00

Jesus Is the Head and We Are the Body
Ephesians 5:21-31

Vs. 23: For the husband is the head of the wife as Christ is the head of the church, his body, and is himself its Savior.

Object: A nail, a golf club and a match.

Good morning, boys and girls. How many of you went back to school this week? *(Let them answer.)* Almost all of you are back in school except for the ones who are not going to school this year. This week is such a fun week because we see all our friends that we have not seen during the summer and some of the new kids that will be our very best friends before the school year is over. How do you like your new teachers? *(Let them answer.)* Teachers can be some pretty nice people, especially at the beginning of the year.

I brought some things along with me this morning that I hope you will learn a lesson from. *(Take out the golf club, the match and the nail.)* I have a riddle for you. What is the same about this match, this nail and this golf club? *(Let them answer.)* All of them have something that we call the same name. *(Give them some hints.)* Do you give up? *(Let them answer.)* This is a pretty tough riddle so let me give you the answer. All three things, the match, the nail and the golf club, have heads. *(Point out where the head is on each one.)* That may sound funny to you, but we call each of these things heads, just like we call your head a head. We strike the head of a match and make fire. We pound the head of a nail, and we hit the golf ball with the head of the club. Your head has a lot of things to do such as think, see, hear, smell, taste, and many others. The head is where the business is done or where the important part of the work begins.

Jesus is also the head. The Bible calls Jesus the head of something that all of us love. Do you know what Jesus is the head of? *(Let them answer.)* Jesus is the head of the Church. St. Paul calls Jesus the head of the Church. Who do you think is the body if Jesus is the head of it? *(Let them answer.)* That's right, we are the body of the Church. Jesus Christ is the Head of the Church and we are the Body of the Church. We go together. Jesus is the head because he is the leader and gives the body direction. We are the body because we follow where Jesus leads us. Jesus taught, and still teaches us, and we learn and do what he says. That is the reason that the Bible calls Jesus the head of the Church. We are the arms, legs, chest, and back of the Church.

The next time you see a nail or a match or a golf club or even when you look at one another, and you look at the heads of one another, I hope you will think about how the Bible teaches that Jesus is the head of the Church, and how we are the body of the Church, and how we work together. Amen.

The Armor of God
Ephesians 6:10-20

Vs. 11: Put on the whole armor of God, that you may be able to stand against the wiles of the devil.

Object: A football uniform with all the equipment.

Good morning, boys and girls. How many of you go to your schools' football games with your parents or friends? Do any of you play football? *(Let them answer.)* Some of you go to the games, and some of you even play football. It's a pretty rough game, isn't it? *(Let them answer.)* Do you ever get hurt playing? *(Let them answer.)* When I watch the games at the stadium or on TV, I always think about what a rough game football is, and how easy it would be to get hurt. Of course, I know that the uniform that each football player wears helps to protect him, and also helps him to be a better player.

Have you ever seen all the parts of a football player's uniform? *(Let them answer.)* I brought one along with me this morning so that you could see all the parts. *(Show each pad and tell them where it goes in the uniform.)* You can see how many different parts it takes to protect the body against injury. There is something for the knee, the hip, the thigh, the ribs, the shoulder and the head. When you are wearing all these pads it means that you can hit harder and you can take harder hits from other football players.

Christians are a little bit like football players. We have to play in a pretty rough world sometimes with people who are not so nice. Some people we know like

74

to lie and do mean things. Others play unfair and cheat while some will do anything to hurt someone else. If you are a Christian, you can't do the same things that they do. We don't want you to lie or steal from someone else and hurt them because you were hurt. A Christian cannot do those kinds of things. That is why St. Paul tells us to help ourselves with a different kind of equipment. Pretend that these shoulder pads are called "forgiveness" and that this helmet is called "truth." We can name the knee pads the "love" that God has for you and the hip pads, "honesty." When you put on all the good things that God has to give you to protect you in this world, then you are safe. I know that some people are going to try and hurt you, and sometimes you will wonder if it is worth being a Christian. But I know that it is, and you will know that it is also when you know how you feel after telling the truth, or after forgiving someone who has tried to hurt you.

Jesus has a special place for the people who wear his kind of protection, and I know that you will want to share what he has for you. The next time you see a football player, remember the kind of pads that God is asking you to wear, and you will know how much he cares for you in this world. God Bless you. Amen.

Anger Doesn't Work!
James 1:17-22, 23-27

Vs. 20: For the anger of man does not work the righteousness of God.

Object: A pitcher of water, a strainer, and an empty bucket.

Good morning, boys and girls. Today I have a small experiment for you, and I hope that by doing it, we will learn something about the ways of God and the ways of people. I brought along with me this pitcher of water and an empty bucket. I need to get the water from this place where the pitcher is, to the empty bucket, without moving either the pitcher or the bucket. I also brought along this thing that we call a strainer to help me get the water out of the pitcher and over to the bucket. Do you think it will work? *(Let them answer.)* You don't think it will work? Why not? *(Let them answer.)* You think it won't work because the strainer has holes in it! Do you want me to try? *(Let them answer.)* Some of you want me to try and others don't want me to try. I am going to try it. *(Begin to pour some of the water into the strainer and run as fast as you can over to the bucket. Let as much as possible fall onto a tray or some object that will take the over flow.)* It didn't work that time, but I am going to try it again. Maybe if I run a little faster. *(Try it again.)* It didn't work that time either so now I am going to try and pour it a little faster. *(Try it once more.)* It just doesn't work. Using a strainer to carry water from a pitcher to a bucket just does not work. Our experiment has failed.

But doing that experiment has taught me something about God and people, and let me tell you what it is. Have you ever heard someone trying to tell someone else about God in an angry voice? Suppose I told you *(Say this in a very angry and loud voice.) God wants you to worship him every Sunday in this church.* Do you hear God speaking, and have you learned something that you will always remember? I could try another one. *(Again in a very loud and angry voice.) Love your father and mother!* How did you like that? Have you learned how loving your Heavenly Father is? Of course not. Some people think that they can teach about their loving God in a very angry way. People don't learn what is right for them according to God through their anger. That is like trying to carry water in a strainer. It just doesn't work.

The next time that you hear someone trying to teach about God in an angry way, you can think about the time I tried to carry water in a strainer. It just doesn't work. If you want someone to know about our God and his love, teach it in a quiet and joyful way. Then people are sure to listen, and when they listen and are not afraid, they will learn. That's what St. Paul said, and I believe that he is right. I hope you do too. God bless you. Amen.

Faith Needs Work
James 2:1-5, 8-10, 14-18

Vs. 17: So faith by itself, if it has no works, is dead.

Object: A calculator.

Good morning, boys and girls. Today we are going to talk about something that all of us need to learn and understand as soon as possible. We are going to talk about faith, and how to make our faith work. How many of you have heard about the word "faith"? *(Let them answer.)* Faith is something that all of us should have and use. Our faith means that if we believe in something enough, something surely will happen. If I believe that God will heal me when I am hurt, then I have faith in God as a healer. If I believe that God will make enough sunshine and rain so that the corn will grow then I have faith that God is a grower. That is faith.

Some people think that they have so much faith that they do not have to do anything because God will do it all. They don't have to worry about anything since God will do everything. A man by the name of James listened carefully to God and gave us some answers about what people are supposed to do as partners with God. He called it working with God.

Let me show you what I mean. I have a calculator. The answer to almost any problem that I can think of that has to do with numbers is in this calculator. If I want to know how much 16 times 16 is I know that the answer is in this calculator. I have faith that the calculator has the answer. Do you think the calculator has the answer? *(Let them answer.)* You think the answer is in there also. Do you think that the answer is right? *(Let them answer.)* You think that the right answer is in the calculator. How are we going to get the right answer out of the calculator? *(Let them answer.)* That's right, we have to push the buttons. If I push 16 and the button for times and then another 16, I will get the answer of 256. That is the correct answer. My faith that the calculator had the right answer in there is good. I can do it again by asking how big is a room 25 feet long and 15 feet wide. The answer is 375 square feet. Again, I have done some work to push the buttons, but my faith that the calculator would give the right answer is correct.

My faith is that God wants everyone to be happy, healthy and have a warm place to live. That is what my faith tells me. But as a Christian I also know that God has given me land to grow food, love to make other people happy and hands to help build warm houses. I can help people to know my God and his love by sharing my life with them. I must do good things, or work to help others know the God that I believe in. Having faith in God is not enough if we don't share our lives and our work to help others know God as well.

When you see a calculator you have faith that the right answers are inside of it. But you must use the buttons, do the work, to get the answers to your problems.

We must believe that God will answer our problems, but we must also do things that let God help us and all our friends. Amen.

Try for a Good Life
James 3:16-4:6

Vs. 3:18: And the harvest of righteousness is sown in peace by those who make peace.

Object: Bricks and raisins.

Good morning, boys and girls. Isn't this beautiful weather we are having at this time of the year? How many of you like fall? *(Let them answer.)* What do you like most about this time of year? *(Let them answer.)* I think I like the warm days and the cool nights and the changing colors in the trees. Even though it is the same thing every year I never grow tired of the beautiful fall days. Lots of things don't change. I brought along with me some things that I found to help me tell you something that I learned from the Bible.

The first thing I have with me is a brick. How many of you know what a brick is used for? *(Let them answer.)* That's right, it is used to build houses. When you build a house with bricks, do you have a wood house? *(Let them answer.)* Of course not. You build a house of bricks, and you have a brick house. Bricks don't change to wood shingles or boards. A house built with brick is a brick house.

I also brought some raisins. I like raisin bread. If the baker uses raisins in his dough and bakes it, then what kind of bread will the baker have when it is finished? *(Let them answer.)* Right, raisin bread. He won't have rye bread or whole wheat bread or just plain white bread when he finishes; he will have raisin bread. That means that whatever he puts into the bread is the kind of bread that he will have when it is baked.

The Bible tells us that the goodness of our lives and the world we live in is a little bit like the brick layer making a house and the baker making bread. Your life will be just as good as the good things you put in it, or just as bad as the bad things that you put in it. Our world will be as good or as bad as the people are that live in it. If you want peace in the world, then you must have peace in your heart. If you want happy and joyful people in the world, then you must be happy and joyful. If you want people who are filled with love and like to share, then you must have love and be ready to share the things that are yours. Our world is made up of people like you and me, and the kind of world we get is the same as what we put into it.

You can't have raisin bread unless you put the raisins in the dough. You can't have a brick house unless you make it with bricks. You can have a good life if you are good. God made his world this way, and it is the best kind of world that I can think of.

You make our world a better world by loving, sharing, forgiving and being joyful. You will also help other people in the world be good and joyful, too. Amen.

Share Your Life
James 4:7-12 [13-5:6]

Vs. 10: Humble yourselves before the Lord and he will exalt you.

Object: Two buckets of water and some Spic and Span and some dirty boards.

Good morning, boys and girls. Today we are going to meet a friend of your mother's, and see why she likes it so much. How many of you ever help your mother clean house? *(Let them answer.)* That is a hard job and one that has to be done over and over. I think mothers are really great the way that they keep our houses clean. Suppose that your mother did not clean your house for a month or maybe a year. What do you think your house would look like? You wouldn't be able to find a thing. It would be buried in newspapers, and in mud off your shoes, if you could find your shoes. All of the dishes would be lost in the garbage of your kitchen, if you could find the kitchen, and your bedroom would be filled with dust, paper, and dirty clothes.

But because we have mothers who care, our homes are different. I brought along a very humble friend of your mother's. You noticed that I said humble. This friend is her cleaning soap. It comes in a powder and can only be used when it gives up its life to become something else. Let me show you what I mean. I brought along some dirty boards and a couple of buckets of water. I am going to try and clean one of the boards with this plain bucket of water. *(Wash the board.)* Not bad, but the board is still dirty. All the dirt did not come off. Now I am going to take a little bit of this powder, the humble friend of your mother, and put it in the other bucket. If you watch very carefully you will see the powder give itself up and disappear in the water. It is something special now. The water has become very powerful and can do things that the other bucket of water could not do. *(Wash another board with the second bucket.)* Look at the difference. The very humble soap and friend of your mother has given up being just a powder and become something very different. It can now clean the dirtiest of boards and make them look like new again.

You can be like this also only in a different way. The Bible teaches us that when we give up our selfish ways, and share our lives with others, and become workers for God, we can become very powerful people who can do many good things. We are like the soap. When we try to stay to ourselves and be selfish, we are not worth very much. But when we give ourselves up to God and get mixed up with all his goodness, then we become very powerful people.

The next time that you see your mother clean house, ask her if she is not using some very humble soap that becomes very powerful when it is mixed with water. Then thank her for making your house such a wonderful clean place to live. Amen.

Jesus Was a Pioneer
Hebrews 2:9-11 [12-18]

Vs. 10: For it was fitting that he, for whom and by whom all things exist, in bringing many sons to glory, should make the pioneer of their salvation perfect through suffering.

Object: An antique that would be representative of the pioneer period of our country such as a butter churn, coonskin cap, a musket or any other item that is easily obtained.

Good morning, boys and girls. How many of you like to see movies about old days? *(Let them answer.)* What do you think about when I say the word "pioneer"? *(Let them answer.)* You think of people like Daniel Boone and Davey Crockett. Do you think about hunting in the woods and living in log cabins? *(Let them answer.)* The people had to make all their own clothes. They wore caps that were made out of animal skins. We call a hat like this a coonskin hat because it was made out of the skin of a raccoon. They had to make their own butter by churning it for many hours in something that looked like this. *(Show them a butter churn.)* They had to hunt all of their food in the woods. To do that, they had to carry these very heavy guns that were called muskets. It was a hard life, but they must have enjoyed living in the wilds and being free to do whatever they wanted to do.

Jesus was a pioneer. The Bible even calls him a pioneer. Jesus lived a life that was different from anyone else's life because he went in new directions that God sent him. Jesus came to do something that had never been done before. He came to save men from their sins. He had to teach new things and show men how life was supposed to be lived *with* God rather than *against* God. That wasn't easy. People don't like to change. People always think that they know best. God wanted people to live free from sin, and so he sent Jesus. God told him to go in a different direction than the way people were living. Many times Jesus had to do something all by himself. There was no one else to help him or share it with him. It was a hard life to live, but one that Jesus really enjoyed. Finally, Jesus was the true pioneer, because he died for our sins. Just like the pioneers made our country safe for us to live in, Jesus made life safe for us after death by dying for our sins. That is why the Bible calls Jesus a pioneer. Jesus died for our sins so that we would never have to worry about dying again, if we believed in his teachings and the love that God wanted to share with us.

The next time you see something that makes you think about pioneers, I hope that you will think about Jesus and the way that he was a pioneer for all of us, and how he died for our sins so that we could live forever in safety with God. Amen.

We Are the Church
Hebrews 3:1-6

Vs. 6b: We are his house if we keep up our courage and our confidence in what we hope for.

Object: Some bricks, wood, a miniature tent.

Good morning, boys and girls. I have some very strange things with me today. *(Show them the bricks, the wood and the tent.)* Why do you suppose I brought these bricks and this wood with me to church? *(Let them guess.)* Well, today we are going to talk about houses. What is your house made of, do you know? *(Let them tell you.)* Your house probably has a lot of wood in it. Maybe it is also made out of brick. Houses are made out of very strong materials so that when the storms and winds come, they won't blow over or get damaged. A long time ago people lived in houses that looked very different from ours. What did the Indians make their houses out of? *(Let them tell you.)* They had houses that looked like tents. They were made of mud and straw and probably even animal skins. If you had been an Indian, you wouldn't have had a very big house, would you? It would have been like living in a tent. *(Hold up the tent.)* There was only one big room and that's where everyone slept and ate and lived. Do you think that you would have liked being an Indian? *(Let them answer.)* What kinds of houses do you suppose the people of Jesus' day lived in? *(Let them guess.)* Some of them were built right into the side of a hill. It would be like living in a cave. The houses of Jesus' day probably weren't very big, either, and they didn't have all the nice things that we have — like garbage disposals and running water and showers and dishwashers and carpet on the floor.

Today's Scripture lesson talks about a very special kind of house — the house of God, the church. This house is very special because it is where we all come together to worship God our Father. This is where we sing his praises and learn more about him each Sunday. Most churches are nice big buildings where all the people can come together. But you know boys and girls, our Scripture tells us something very unusual about the church. It says that the church isn't really made of brick or stone or wood. Can you guess what the church is really made out of? *(Let them guess.)* The church is made of *people!* You and I and your moms and dads and brothers and sisters and aunts and uncles and neighbors — all of us are the church. That means that even if this building weren't here, we would still have a church. The church isn't made up of things — it is made up of people who follow Jesus. You and I are really God's house. That is a very wonderful thought, isn't it, boys and girls? That means that we have to be the very best kind of house we can be — a house that is better than all of the lovely churches all over the world. Today as we worship God in this building, let's remember the special message of our Scripture lesson: We are all God's people — God's house — the church! God bless you. Amen.

God Sees Right Through
Hebrews 4:9-16

Vs. 13: And before him no creature is hidden, but all are open and laid bare to the eyes of him with whom we have to do.

Object: A big piece of clear plastic used to cover many or all of the children.

Good morning, boys and girls. Today we are going to find something out about God and something about ourselves. Have you ever done something that you were really ashamed of? *(Let them answer.)* You don't have to tell me what it was, but I want you to think about it. When you have thought about his awful thing that you did or the stupid thing that you did that makes you ashamed, then just raise your hand. *(Wait for a few hands to be put up before moving to the next part.)* When you feel ashamed or embarrassed for something you have done, you feel like hiding, don't you? *(Let them answer.)* Of course you do. You wish that no one could see you. If there was any place to hide, you would like to hide.

I guess that is the way we should feel when we commit any sin. Some people stay away from coming to worship services when they have done some sin that they think is really awful. They try to hide from God.

Let's pretend that all of us have done some pretty awful things, and we want to hide from our parents. I am going to help you hide so that no one here today will see you. I brought along a big covering that I will put over the top of all of you. You stay under it and be pretty quiet and no one will know that you are here. *(Take out the plastic covering.)* Now think about the stupid thing that you did or that pretty awful thing that you don't want anyone to know about while I am covering you. *(Put the plastic covering over them.)*

Is everyone covered? *(Let them answer.)* Do you feel better now that you are hidden? Are you glad that no one can see how embarrassed or sorry you feel? *(Let them answer.)* I don't think anyone here can see you, do you? *(Let them answer.)* That's right of course, they can see you. everyone here can see right through the plastic covering that I put over you.

That's the same way it is with God. People try to hide their sins from God, and they think that they are doing a pretty good job of it. But they are only kidding themselves. You can't hide from God in his world no matter where you are. God sees and knows everything about us. Amen.

The Source of Life
Hebrews 5:1-10

Vs. 9: And being made perfect he became the source of eternal salvation to all who obey him.

Object: Some milk and a picture of a cow.

Good morning, boys and girls. Last week I talked to you about my cat and a needle, and this morning I want to talk to you about another animal. Last week I didn't have a camel so I had to bring my cat. This week I want to talk to you about a cow. Does that look like a cow to you? *(Let them answer.)* That's good because it is the only picture of a cow that I could find. Why do we like cows so much? What does a cow do for all of us? *(Let them answer.)* That's right, a cow gives us the milk that we drink, put on our cereal, and use in our cooking. Cows are great. If you like milk, maybe you would like to make all the cows all over America feel good this morning by giving them a cheer. Let's do it, are you ready? Hip, hip, hooray, hip, hip, hooray!!! I just know that made all the cows feel a lot better.

The real reason that I brought this picture, though, was to help you learn something about Jesus. A cow is the source of our milk. Did you hear that special word. The special word is source. A cow is the source of milk. That means that milk comes from a cow.

A cow is a source for milk like Jesus is our source of salvation. We are saved by Jesus. Because Jesus did what he did, we will live forever. That is really important. It is even more important than what the cow does. Jesus lived and died for us so that we could live forever. If Jesus had not done what he did, we would not have any life after we died here on earth. It is because of Jesus that we have something really special to look forward to after we die.

The Bible calls Jesus the source. The Bible tells us that when Jesus died he did something very special or made something very special that forgives us all our sins. We don't have to worry about making something special for God or paying him back in any way. We just tell God how grateful we are for his son Jesus and how much we love him; God promises us a place in his world after we die in this world.

The word is "source." Jesus is our source of eternal life. A cow is our source for milk. Jesus is our source for life. That is really special to think about and remember. Jesus and cows are both the source of something good but Jesus is the most precious source of all. Amen.

A Bolt, a Nut, and a Washer
Hebrews 7:23-28

Vs. 25: Consequently he is able for all time to save those who draw near to God through him, and since he always lives to make intercession for them.

Object: A nut, a bolt and a washer.

Good morning, boys and girls. Today, we are talking about a very big word, and also a very important one. The word is "intercession." What do you think the word intercession might mean? *(Let them answer.)* Those were all good tries, but they are not the answers. I said it was a big word and not one that we use very often. I think that I can help you learn what it means in just a minute. First of all, I want to tell you that Jesus is our intercession. That will help us to learn more about what the word means.

I brought with me a bolt that you might use when you are building a table, or chair, or almost anything. Sometimes when you are building something, it is necessary to drill a hole and use a bolt. But when you use a bolt, you must also use a nut. The nut just twists right on the bolt and helps to hold something together. There is one thing missing if you want to keep the bolt and nut from pulling right through the wood. You need a washer, something to come between the bolt and the nut.

Now here is where you must pretend. Let's say that the bolt is God, and we are the nut. God wants you and me to be close together but because we are not always good and right, we have some problems with God. Our problems are called sins. We just don't belong in the same place with a very holy God. God wants us, and we want God, but because God is pure and holy we don't belong together. Jesus is the washer. Jesus comes between God and us just like the washer is in between the bolt and the nut. Jesus makes us fit good with God because Jesus takes all our sins and gets rid of them. Jesus listens to God the Father just like he listens to us, and he brings us together. We fit better because of Jesus, just like the bolt and nut fit together because of the washer.

The washer comes between and is called the intercessor or intercession. He listens and works for both sides.

That is why Jesus is so important to you and to me. He speaks for us and acts for us with God the Father. Jesus also speaks for God the Father and acts for God the Father. He is the intercession. We pray to God the Father through the name of Jesus, and God gives us forgiveness through his Son Jesus Christ.

Intercession is a big word and a very important one to all of us. When you pray, you use the name of Jesus who speaks to the Father for us. A bolt, a nut and a washer help us to understand the way that God works with us through Jesus. Amen.

I Am the Beginning and the End
Revelation 1:4b-8

Vs. 8: "I am the Alpha and the Omega," says the Lord God, who is and who was and who is to come, the Almighty.

Object: A step ladder.

Good morning, boys and girls. Today is the Last Sunday in the season of Pentecost. This means that this Sunday is the last Sunday in the Church Year. Next week will be like New Year's Day in the church. Pentecost is our longest season and during that time of almost twenty-six weeks we learn a lot about the ministry of Jesus when he lived here on the earth. We have talked about his teachings, his miracles, the stories that he told and something about his family and friends and the places that he lived and worked. We have also learned a lot about people like Paul, John, Peter, and many others. Today, we have some verses from the book of Revelation where Jesus, the Christ, says that he is the beginning and the end of everything. He is the first and the last, or the A and the Z of the alphabet. In other words, there is nothing before Jesus and there will not be anything after him.

Let me show you what I mean. I brought along with me a step ladder. You are able to do a lot of things with a step ladder. You can wash walls, paint houses, clean cupboards, change light bulbs and lots of things like this. It has steps. It has a first step and a last step. There are no steps before the first step and there are no steps after the last step. If you have to reach above the last step, you are going to do what? *(Let them answer.)* That's right, you are going to fall. If you wanted to step before the first step, there is what? *(Let them answer.)* That's right, nothing. The ladder has a first step and it has a last step. There is the beginning and the end of the ladder.

So that is the way it is with Jesus. He wanted everyone to know that he was there before the world was made. He was there when the Father created the heavens and the earth, the land and the sea. He was there when the Father created people. He was with all of the great heroes like Abraham and David, and he has been with all of the heroes and their people ever since. Now Jesus is telling us he is going to be with us to the very end, to the last. There is nothing beyond the Christ.

The next time you see a ladder and you look at the steps and you see that there is a first step and there is a last step, maybe you will think about Jesus and how he has always been with us and always will be with us. Jesus said, I am the beginning and the end. Amen.

How to Be a Christian
1 Thessalonians 3:9-13

Vs. 10: Praying earnestly night and day that we may see you face to face and supply what is lacking in your faith?

Object: Some boards, nails and hammers, or screws and screwdrivers.

Good morning, boys and girls. How many of you have ever started to do a job, but when you were ready to start, you found that you were missing something? *(Let them answer.)* Let me show you what I mean. Let's pretend that we want to put these nails in the board. You have the nails and you have the board, now put the nails in it. *(Hold back the hammer.)* Who wants to put the nails in? *(Ask for a volunteer but do not give him a hammer.)* What's the problem? Can't you put the nails into the board? Do you need something else? *(Let them answer.)* That's right, you need a hammer. You can't do the job unless you have a hammer, can you?

The same thing would be true if I gave you a board and some screws. If you did not have a screwdriver, you could not put the screws into the board. You need all of the proper tools to do a job right. St. Paul knew the same thing was true about Christians. He wrote to some of his friends and told them how much he was praying for them and how happy he was for them to be Christians. But he did not stop there. St. Paul knew that it took a lot of parts to make a whole Christian, and he wanted to see his friends so he could teach them all he knew about being a Christian.

Sometimes we have that same problem. We call

ourselves Christians, but we have not learned all the parts about being a Christian. We need to learn to love and forgive as well as to worship and share. We cannot be jealous or cheat, steal, lie, or any of the other things that aren't Christian. When we do commit our sins we must go to God and ask for his forgiveness.

St. Paul wanted to tell his friends how to be a whole Christian and show them how real Christians live. You and I want to do the same thing with our friends. We want them to be Christians, and full Christians. We want to share the things that we do well, and we want them to share with us the things that they do well. It is a good plan and everybody should support it.

You can't drive nails into a board without a hammer, and you can't be a full Christian without prayer of love or sharing your riches. That is what St. Paul shared with his friends and it is the same thing that he shares with us today.

Share what you have and what you know with your friends, and both of you will be stronger Christians tomorrow. Amen.

A Great Partnership
Philippians 1:3-11

Vs. 5: Thankful for your partnership in the gospel from the first day until now.

Object: Salt and pepper.

Good morning, boys and girls. Today we are going to talk about some really good friends. They have been partners for a long time. I am sure that many of you have seen them together, as a matter of fact, you have probably never seen one without the other. In case you have not met them, I want to be the first to introduce the great partnership of salt and pepper. Day after day they do a job on my food. In the morning I eat eggs, and the first thing I do is put a little salt and some pepper on them. At noon I like to eat a salad, and I immediately reach for the partners — salt and pepper. Then at night when it is time for dinner, and I sit down to my vegetables and potatoes, I have, of course, the all-time favorite, salt and pepper. They work so well together. You can always count on them to add a little spice to your life. Salt and pepper, a great partnership and one that I would not be without.

There are lots of partnerships, some just as good as salt and pepper and some not so good. One of the best partnerships that I heard about was between St. Paul and the people at Philippi. The people of Philippi were always helpful to St. Paul when he carried his message of Jesus to the world. They supported him with gifts and prayers, and they welcomed him to their city when he was in the area. They loved Paul because of his ministry and the way that he shared his knowledge of Jesus. He could sit there for hours and tell them the good news that Jesus brought to them, and how he loved them so much that he even died for them. They also were glad to take his teachings and share them with other people in other cities. It was a wonderful partnership that Paul had with the people of Philippi. Once when the Romans put Paul in prison for teaching about Jesus as God, the people of Philippi came to defend him and support him. They knew that Paul had not done anything wrong, and they were willing to stand by him with their love. It was as St. Paul said, a great partnership, and I know that you would have been just as glad to have friends like the Philippians as St. Paul was.

The next time you hear of a partnership, you can think of St. Paul and the people in Philippi. Perhaps you will think of him this noon when you eat lunch and you look at the table and see that great partnership of salt and pepper. If you do see it, think about the time that Paul's partners, the Philippians, stood by him when he was in trouble. Will you do that? That's wonderful. Amen.

Make a List for God
Philippians 4:4-7

Vs. 6: Have no anxiety about anything, but in everything by prayer and supplication with thanksgiving let your requests be made known to God.

Object: Your Christmas shopping list, or, if you want, call it the list for Santa Claus.

Good morning, boys and girls. It seems to me that there is something special in the air. We must be getting close to something, but I haven't figured out yet what it is. Does anyone here know of anything that we are getting close to that I don't know about? *(Let them answer.)* Christmas, that's right. What day does Christmas come on? *(Let them answer.)* The twenty-fifth of December. That is only nine days away. I know I have something here to remind me about Christmas, but I have forgotten what it is. *(Search your pockets until you come up with your shopping list.)* Here it is, my shopping list. Now I remember, this is the time of the year when I buy presents for all my family and many of my friends. I have something to buy for each member of my family. Are they going to be surprised. Do you make out a list like this or have your mother or dad make out a list for you? *(Let them answer.)* I thought so. Some of the best fun is making out the list.

God likes lists also. Did you know that God liked for you to make out lists for him? *(Let them answer.)* That's true. As a matter of fact, when St. Paul was talking to the people of Philippi, he told them that they should keep lists of things that they wanted to ask or share with God, and then tell him about them when they prayed. That's a good idea. We could all keep lists of the things that we want to talk over with God. Paul said that some of the things could be requests, that means things that we need from God. There are a lot of things that only God can give, and we should let him know about them.

Suppose that we were going to make a list today of the things that we wanted to ask God. I wonder what they would be. I probably would not ask God for a ten-speed bicycle, but I think that I would ask him for some extra-special love to share with the mean old man who lives across the street from me. I know I don't have enough love by myself and only God could give me enough love to love that mean man. If I loved him really good, then maybe he would not be so mean to anyone anymore. What would you ask from God if you could write out a list? *(Let them answer.)* Those are some pretty good things to ask God for, and I hope that you will think about them not only today, but every day. Lists for Christmas are great, but you can only ask for those things once a year. When you make out lists to ask God, you can ask him every day. That's pretty great. I think so and so do all Christians that love him and share him with each other. Amen.

A Time for Giving
Hebrews 10:5-10

Vs. 10: And by that will we have been sanctified through the offering of the body of Jesus Christ once for all.

Object: A very pretty package, wrapped like a Christmas package.

Good morning, boys and girls. Today I have a very special problem that I need to share with you. I have heard about children your age all over the world who will have a very different Christmas than the kind that you are going to have. These children are called refugees. Does anyone know what the word refugee means? *(Let them answer.)* That's right, a refugee is someone who no longer has a home. Most of the time that refugee doesn't have clothes, food and perhaps even parents or relatives. Most of the time refugees are the result of war. There are millions of refugees in the world today, and while we are getting ready for one of the best Christmases we have ever had, the refugees will try to stay alive for another day. We are going to have all kinds of presents, food and new clothes given to us the day after tomorrow. Christmas day. I was wondering if any of us would be willing to make a sacrifice in the name of Jesus' birthday and give something that we have gotten for Christ's birthday to a refugee child? I think that it would be a wonderful time for us to consider making a sacrifice.

The Scripture lesson today talks about the coming of Christ and how he is born into our world as a sacrifice for us. Jesus came to save us from our sins, and he was born to die for us. That was the most important sacrifice the world has ever known. He died to be a sacrifice once and for all for everyone's sins. He taught us how important it was to sacrifice ourselves for one another. Jesus gave his life for us.

There are millions of people who have no help. They have little food, and so they have no strength to work and no place to work. They live out in the field, a field, with maybe a tent over their head. The only clothes they have are the rags that they escaped with and those will not last long. Christmas is a wonderful time for us, but it is also a time when we might learn how important the sacrifice of Jesus was by making a small sacrifice ourselves.

When you go home today, you may want to talk to your parents about making a sacrifice this Christmas so that another child just like you some place else in the world will also be reminded of the gift Jesus gave with his life. Amen.

Jesus Our Brother
Hebrews 2:10-18

Vs. 11: For he who sanctifies and those who are sanctified have all one origin. That is why he is not ashamed to call them brethren.

Object: A group of ball point pens and one very special ball point pen.

Good morning, boys and girls. Christmas day is over, but we are still celebrating the birthday of Jesus. What a wonderful time all of us had on Christmas. What did you like most about Christmas? *(Let them answer.)* Did you remember to wish Jesus a happy birthday? *(Let them answer.)* I know that you would want to wish your brother a happy birthday if he had a birthday so I am sure that you did the same for Jesus. Did you know that Jesus is our brother? *(Let them answer.)* That's right. The Bible talks about Jesus as our brother. We are God's children, aren't we? *(Let them answer.)* Of course we are. And the Bible talks about Jesus as being the son of God, doesn't it? *(Let them answer.)* It certainly does. So if we are sons and daughters of God and Jesus is the Son of God then that makes Jesus our brother, doesn't it? *(Let them answer.)*

I brought along some pens to show you what I mean. Here are some beautiful pens. There are a lot of different colors, but they all write, and they are all pens, aren't they? *(Let them answer.)* Some are blue and they have black ink, and some are red and they have blue ink, and some are yellow and they have red ink, but they are all pens. There is one pen that is sort

of special. Can you see the one that I mean? It looks a
little different from the rest but it has ink and it writes.
I call this my Jesus pen. All the other pens are people
pens like you and me. But we all write and we all have
ink and we are all pens. Jesus is different because he
is perfect and because he died for our sins. But he is
our brother and he is not ashamed of us. Jesus was
human, fully human. He had hair and eyes and he ate
food and he walked and talked and did everything that
we can do. Jesus is our brother. Jesus could do some
special things that we cannot do but that doesn't
mean that he is not our brother.

That is why the Bible says that even though Jesus
is special, he is not embarrassed or ashamed to have
you and me as his brothers and sisters. What a
wonderful plan God had to send Jesus to us and let
him be our brother.

The next time you take a look at a bunch of pens, or
you see a special pen that is a little different from the
ordinary pen, I hope that you will remember this story
about how Jesus came to live with us and called
himself our brother. I know that I will, and I hope that
you will also. God bless you and have a very happy day.
Amen.